Colonial Philippines in Italian Travel Writing

The first comprehensive review of all extant "Italian" chronicles set in the Philippine Islands, this book juxtaposes "Filipino" Otherness with the unique condition of "Italian" ambivalence and alterity within Europe.

This book's contribution to the critical studies of travel is the opening of an analytical middle ground, highlighting the ambivalence of Italian chroniclers while acknowledging their participation in epistemological practices subsumed within the broader enterprise of conquest.

Beyond the role of travel writing in colonial episteme, the book also situates the act of writing about one's travels in instances of national character building (in Italy's case) and in attempts of constructing a national historiography (in the Philippines' case). This manner of nuancing literary productions by the West while navigating its implications in the East, specifically, how pre-Unification "Italian" travel informed nationalist constructions in the Revolutionary Philippines, could enrich our understanding of and refract monolithic conceptions of metropole–periphery relations.

Jillian Loise Melchor is Assistant Professor and Italian Section Coordinator of the Department of European Languages of the University of the Philippines Diliman. She was a former faculty member of the Division of Humanities of UP Visayas where she taught Spanish, literary translation, and cultural studies. Her master's degree in multilingual cultural studies was funded by the Erasmus Mundus academic council and was obtained from the Universities of Sheffield (UK), Bergamo (Italy), and Santiago de Compostela (Spain). She is currently doing her doctoral research on the decolonisation of creole language heritage as an EDUFI (Finnish National Agency for Education) fellow at the University of Helsinki's Department of Languages. She is a published literary translator and has international, peer-reviewed publications examining the link between language and power in fields such as multilingual heritage, language education policy, and postcolonial linguistics.

Routledge Focus on Literature

Contemporary Irish Masculinities
Male Homosociality in Sally Rooney's Novels
Angelos Bollas

Creative Writing and the Experiences of Others
Strategies for Outsiders
Nandita Dinesh

Emotionality
Heterosexual Love and Emotional Development in Popular Romance
Eirini Arvanitaki

Digital Culture and the Hermeneutic Tradition
Suspicion, Trust, and Dialogue
Inge van de Ven and Lucie Chateau

Dreams in Chinese Fiction
Spiritism, Aestheticism, and Nationalism
Johannes D. Kaminski

Remapping Energopolitics
Blue Humanities, Geophilosophy and Sri Lankan Minor Writings
Abhisek Ghosal

Colonial Philippines in Italian Travel Writing
"Italians" Interpreting Difference
Jillian Loise Melchor

For more information about this series, please visit: www.routledge.com/Routledge-Focus-on-Literature/book-series/RFLT

Colonial Philippines in Italian Travel Writing

“Italians” Interpreting Difference

Jillian Loise Melchor

NEW YORK AND LONDON

First published 2024
by Routledge
605 Third Avenue, New York, NY 10158

and by Routledge
4 Park Square, Milton Park, Abingdon, Oxon, OX14 4RN

Routledge is an imprint of the Taylor & Francis Group, an informa business

ISBN: 978-1-032-72192-7 (hbk)
ISBN: 978-1-032-72230-6 (pbk)
ISBN: 978-1-032-72232-0 (ebk)

DOI: 10.4324/9781032722320

Typeset in Times New Roman
by Apex CoVantage, LLC

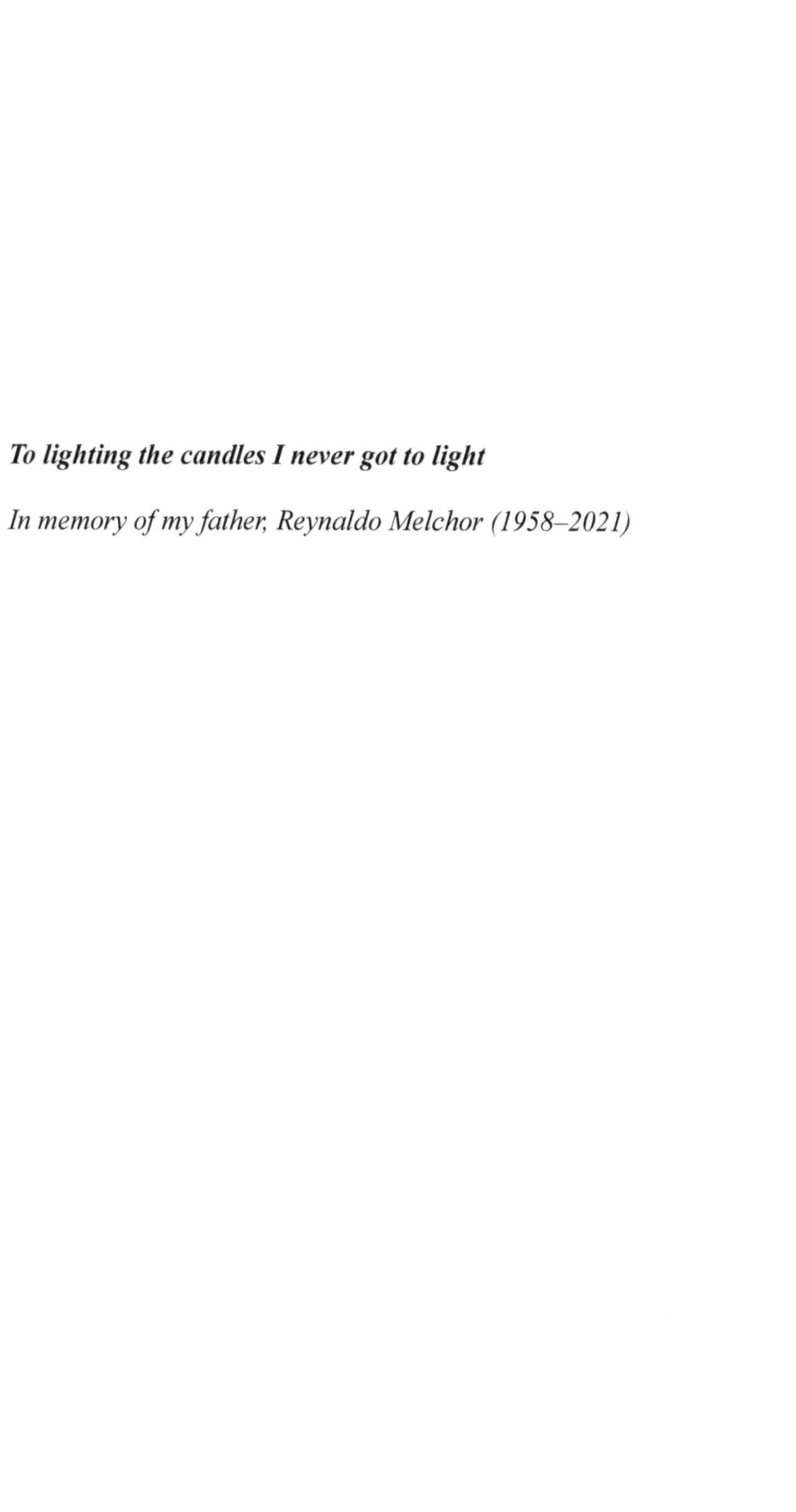

To lighting the candles I never got to light

In memory of my father, Reynaldo Melchor (1958–2021)

Contents

Acknowledgements

This would not have been written without the valuable help and immeasurable patience of colleagues, mentors, family, and friends.

For inspiring me to write about the official chronicler of the first voyage around the world, I am thankful to Emanuela Adesini. For his insights and thoroughness, I thank Tomas Espino Barrera.

For gleefully reading the earliest iterations of this research, I thank you wholeheartedly, Jonathan Bennett (1966–2022).

For always lending me her fresh eyes, I thank my sister, Jenina Danielle Melchor.

For the unparalleled support and for pushing me to give shape to my often-amorphous ideas, I am forever grateful to Miguel Blázquez-Carretero.

This work has been honed over the years thanks to dialogues with colleagues from different corners of the globe. In a way, the writing and research process from which this book emerges can be qualified, too, as itinerant. I am indebted to the exhaustive and incisive comments of scholars who read the monograph proposal, particularly Ernest Rafael Hartwell (Western Washington University) and Tom Sykes (University of Portsmouth). I thank Wystan de la Peña (University of the Philippines Diliman) for his longstanding encouragement.

Lastly, I am grateful to have the support of my families around the world. Salamat sa aking pamilya sa Maynila, lalo na sa aking inang si Marjorie Melchor at sa aking mga bunsong kapatid na sina Ani at Janelle. Agyamanak kadagiti kabagyan mi aglalo na kadagidi kakabsat ti amang ko dita California. A mi familia en Ávila, os doy mil gracias por el apoyo en estos últimos años.

Introduction

The year 2021 marked the 500th anniversary of the Spanish-backed enterprise that would come to be famed as the "first voyage around the world." The Magellan-Elcano expedition bears a heavy weight in history not only because it marked the first successful circumnavigation of the globe, doubtless an astounding feat of geographic and maritime technology, but also because it signalled the "discovery" and subsequent colonisation of the Philippine Islands. Their audacious journey was chronicled by an inquisitive man of letters from the Italian peninsula. Having survived previously uncharted waters and tension-filled encounters, Antonio Pigafetta had the occasion to narrate his marvelous travels to the high courts of Europe, which were extremely fascinated by the "heroic dimensions of [his account's] incredible historical subject" (Cachey Jr., 2007: xii). In 1525, a quintessential travelogue lent itself to the prying eyes of history. Inspired by Renaissance courtly literature, the aptly titled "Primo viaggio intorno al globo terracqueo."[1] 'First voyage around the globe' would come to represent the early modern European urge to explore and confront the Other.

The COVID-19 pandemic unfortunately pushed back various academic and artistic endeavours to commemorate the momentous East–West encounter that was the Magellan–Elcano expedition. Thus, it is still an opportune time to interrogate and nuance the extensive body of colonial-era travel writing that irrevocably shaped global history. It is here where the general aim of this book is situated. Chronicles about the Philippine archipelago, produced from the onset of its colonisation to its eventual independence, remain a fertile ground for critical elaboration. The corpus is vast and the possible lines of inquiry innumerable. Echoing the still relevant sentiment of a Filipino historian and literary critic, there remains an "impulse to subject to closer scrutiny topics which may be 'familiar' but have been dealt with only in part or in a general way in previous studies" (Mojares, 1981: 309). In this book, we narrow the scope of investigation to colonial-era travel accounts written by Italian voyagers, employing an interdisciplinary approach to historiography as we draw

DOI: 10.4324/9781032722320-1

from critical theory and literary history to scrutinise itinerant knowledge production in the early Modern period. Much scholarship on colonial-era travel to the Philippine archipelago treats chronicles as historical sources while the literary qualities and inspirations of these texts either recede into the background or are altogether overlooked.[2] An intersectional theoretical framework weaving together historiography, literary history, and postcolonial criticism could help expand the critical horizons of investigating Europe's and the Asia Pacific's interwoven histories.

Why give special focus to Italian travel writers? Broadly speaking, the Italians are "arguably the most 'well traveled' of the Western European literary traditions" (Cachey, 1996: 55). From Dante's allegorical voyage to the Underworld to Marco Polo's influential peregrination down the Silk Road, Italian literature can hardly be divorced from travel. Indeed, the world owes tales from the so-called Age of Discovery to the quill of many an Italian explorer. Among these chroniclers were the Vicenza-born Antonio Pigafetta (1480–1531), the Florentine Francesco Carletti (1573–1636), and the Calabrian Giovanni Francesco Gemelli Careri (1651–1725), hailing respectively from the northern, central, and southern regions of a linguistically, culturally, and politically fragmented "Italy." All three reached the shores of the Philippine archipelago at different junctures. Pigafetta, the official chronicler of the previously mentioned Magellan–Elcano expedition (1519–1522), hailed from a city that formed part of *La Serenissima*, the robust maritime Republic of Venice, and encountered the Islands on the cusp of colonisation. Magellan's crew hopped from one "*isola desabitata*" 'uninhabited island' (Pigafetta, 1956: 45) to another only to find potential subjects of the King of Spain and heathens in "need" of evangelising. Pigafetta's testimony thus bore witness to Western "discovery" of the archipelago. Carletti and Gemelli Careri, each embarking on a prodigious journey as individual travellers, came across an already consolidated colony. The Florentine merchant Carletti, a subject of the Grand Duchy of Tuscany, is often touted as the first private traveller to have circumnavigated the globe (1594–1602). He witnessed a vibrant Manila in 1596, the centre of the Spanish East Indies that was bustling with trade and rife with ethnic and political tensions. Another self-funded traveller, journeying by land and sea neither for politics nor profit (1693–1698), Gemelli Careri originated from the Kingdom of Naples under the Spanish Crown. In 1696, he set foot on another imperial Spanish holding, Manila, which was then home to "major institutions of temporal and spiritual power" (Manzano, 2013: 107) and, most importantly for the Calabrian globetrotter, a viable gateway to the Americas.

Despite the near-century gap between their voyages, could these accounts display similarities in their portrayal of native domains? What could explain the observable parallelisms or the differences that arise in their descriptions of the inhabitants of that far-flung archipelago, "*quei barbari*" 'those barbarians'

(Carletti, 1958: 82) borne of the islands "*che sono poco conosciute in Europa e meno notate sulle carte geografiche*" 'relatively unknown in Europe and less observed on maps' (Gemelli Careri, 1700: 34)? Yet every traveller has a point of departure and a place of destination. What, then, of their homeland? Do these chroniclers talk about their *patria*, their city or place of origin? And what of their peninsula of provenance, to what extent do they refer to Italy as their homeland? The first comprehensive review of all extant 'Italian' chronicles set in the Philippine Islands, this book merges two hitherto separate lines of inquiry in the examination of colonialist travel writing by juxtaposing "Filipino" Otherness with the unique condition of "Italian" alterity. There exists an academic focus on travel of Italian origin across history, ranging from the pre-Columbian era to the Renaissance all the way to the fascist period and then to contemporary Italian diaspora.[3] There is also ample investigation of the postcolonial implications of travel narratives from consolidated empires, such as the Orientalist tropes in Anglo-Saxon travel writing set in Manila (Sykes, 2022), imperial nostalgia in Spanish travel literature set in China (Ai, 2014), the Portuguese "discovery" of the Far East (Ng, 2022), Hispanic travel writing as an imperial literary instrument (Johnson, 2004), and so forth. Yet the contribution to the geographic imaginary of Empire of explorers from a land deemed merely "a geographical expression"[4] in the eyes of modern Europe has only been adumbrated in travel writing studies and in Italian literary scholarship. A thorough investigation of colonial Philippines as codified in Italian travel redresses such a gap.

But before we can begin our contrapuntal reading of Italian travel literature, we must first deconstruct the genre of travel itself in its distinct historical and contextual iterations, that is, in the broader colonial project, in specific national discourses, and in the ensuing bibliographic evolution and reception of the travel chronicles under scrutiny. As it probes the place of itinerant knowledge production in colonial history, this book addresses thematic and theoretical lacunae observable both in Philippine historiography and in the broad field of Italian literary history. How then does this study proceed framing Italian travel writing against the backdrop of Philippine colonisation, on one hand, and the ambivalent Italian positionality on the other?

First, we problematise *travel writing* as a literary designation and situate the act of writing about one's travels in instances of national character building (in Italy's case) and in attempts of constructing a national historiography (in the Philippine case). From the general, we move into the specific by discussing the different motives of the three chroniclers for embarking on a voyage overseas. Since textual production is what qualifies them as chroniclers and not mere travellers, the bibliographic history of the three travel accounts will be tackled, alongside their reception in early modern European society, on one hand, and in contemporary Philippine scholarship, on the other hand. Lastly, we shall scrutinise the chroniclers' framing of the "Filipino" Other against the notion of the Italian subject's condition of European Otherness.

The opening chapter frames travel writing within the colonial project, zeroes in on the corpus, and discusses the state of the art in the study of Italian travel and that of colonial travel to the Philippines. Here, we ease the reader into the scholarly lacunae that the study seeks to fill in. The second chapter sketches the role of itinerant knowledge in the construction of a national discourse. It argues that intellectual cosmopolitanism propagated through travel writing occupied a central place in the construction of a *coscienza d'italianità* 'consciousness of being Italian' (Croce, 1943: 27) in pre-Unification Italy and in the revolutionary project of creating a "Filipino" identity contra Spanish colonisation. We here suggest that a Gramscian reading of the Filipino intellectual movement in the late nineteenth century can effectively disrupt the coloniser–colonised binary by highlighting the deployment of Western thought in service of imagining and constructing the pre- and postcolonial nation. Before delving deeper into Philippine intellectual engagement with the three Italian chronicles, it is first necessary to contextualise their narratives by interrogating each one's motives for travel.

The third chapter begins with a discussion of the reconfiguration of travel in early modern Europe's changing political and cultural zeitgeist. An in-depth examination of the unique impetus that drove each Italian voyager to set forth on a global journey follows. To gain an insight on Pigafetta's, Carletti's, and Gemelli Careri's motives for travelling, it is imperative to contemplate them as educated subjects in an era where travel represented a pedagogic tool to the individual (Monga, 1996: 19) and an instrument of commerce and conquest to continental powers (Leed, 1991: 159). The widening of the individual's intellectual horizons is thus intimately bound with the continent's geographical expansion. Contextualising travel as journey paves the way for the following chapters which aim to scrutinise travel as text.

In the fourth chapter, the reader would come to see how the distinct historical and political configurations in which the three Italian chronicles emerged, as manifest in their diverging linguistic and rhetorical qualities, would play a role in the publication and reception of each travelogue. Here, pertinent details are provided concerning each text's bibliographic history, exhibiting how the (re)production of travel as text can be as arduous as travel itself as journey. The publication history of each travelogue reveals the waxing and waning discursive value of Italian travel writing in early modern European society. This is accompanied by a discussion of Philippine scholarly engagement with Italian travel literature. The last chapter teases out the similarities and differences in the three "Italian" chroniclers' semiotic creation of the "Filipino" colonised subjects, while carefully accounting for the spatial and temporal divergences between their travels. The key novelty of this reading is the proposal of a counterpoint to postcolonial interpretations of Italian travel narrative that disregard the ambivalent subjectivity of "Italian" travellers as liminal figures themselves, whose pursuit of knowledge and textual production were valuable to the Empire but whose lack of a national origin cast them as outsiders.

This book's contribution to the critical studies of travel shall be the opening of an analytical middle ground, highlighting the ambivalence of Italian chroniclers while acknowledging their participation in epistemological practices subsumed within the broader enterprise of conquest. Put simply, this study explores how the "Italian" chronicler, documenting their travels in the Age of Exploration, shifts his positionality from Othered to Othering.

Notes

1 The original manuscript bears the following title: "*Primo viaggio intorno al globo terracqueo ossia ragguaglio della navigazione alle Indie Orientali per la via d'Occidente fatta sulla squadra del Capit. Magaglianes negli anni 1519–1522*".
2 See Churchill (2016) for an evaluative review of Philippine historiography.
3 For a comprehensive volume on the political and ideological implications of Italian travel to the East in post-Unification Italy (a long period that covers the *Risorgimento* movement, the establishment of the Kingdom of Italy, and Mussolini's fascist rule), see Falcucci et al. (2022).
4 "Prince Metternich, Chancellor of the Austrian Empire and the stoutet champion of the *status quo* in Restoration Europe, dismissed the national aspirations of the Italians by defining Italy as a 'geographical expression'" (Rossi, 1973: 159).

Reference List

Cachey, T. J. (1996). An Italian literary history of travel. *Annali d'Italianistica, 14*, 55–64.
Carletti, F. (1958). *Ragionamenti del mio viaggio al mondo*. Giulio Einaudi editore.
Croce, B. (1943). *Pagine sparse* (Vol. 3). Ricciardi.
Gemelli Careri, G. F. (1700). *Giro del mondo del dottor d. Gio. Francesco Gemelli Careri* (Vol. 5, *contenente le cose più ragguardevoli vedute nell'Isole*). Giuseppe Roselli.
Johnson, C. B. (2004). *(Re)writing the empire: The philippines and filipinos in the hispanic cultural field, 1880–1898* [Doctoral dissertation, The University of Texas at Austin]. UT Electronic Theses and Dissertations. http://hdl.handle.net/2152/1338
Leed, E. J. (1991). *The mind of the traveller. From Gilgamesh to global tourism*. Basic Books.

Manzano, D. (2013). Gemelli and his travel to the philippines. *Asian Perspectives in the Arts and Humanities*, *3*(1), 101–122. https://core.ac.uk/outputs/235946549?source=oai

Mojares, R. B. (1981). Recent Philippine historiography: An evaluative review. *Philippine Quarterly of Culture and Society*, *9*(4), 309–319.

Monga, L. (1996). Travel and travel writing: An historical overview of hodoeporics. *Annali d'italianistica*, *14*, 6–54.

Ng, S. F. (2022). *Writing about discovery in the early modern East Indies*. Cambridge University Press. https://doi.org/10.1017/9781009047029

Pigafetta, A. (1956). Relazione del primo viaggio intorno al mondo. In C. Manfroni (Ed.), *Collana Viaggi Esplorazioni Scoperte*. Istituto editoriale italiano. Original work published 1521.

Sykes, T. (2022). The making of a supranational stereotype: Western literary constructions of the Chinese in Manila and beyond. *Interventions*, *24*(2), 263–283. https://doi.org/10.1080/1369801X.2020.1863839

1 The place of ("Italian") travel writing in the colonial project

Travel writing has always been a key resource in the perennially difficult task to understand, interpret, and reconstruct the interconnected histories brought about by Western engagements with and incursions into far-flung territories. After all, the act of travel was a prerequisite to conquest while the codification of travel served to legitimise conquest. The latter transpired through the circulation and consumption in the metropole of "discourses of difference" (Mills, 2003) formulated within and about the periphery by Western observers. These observers, educated and trained in various professions, were also missionaries, men of science, soldiers, merchants, literary writers, journalists, and at times simply curious folk who had the means to journey from the centre to the fringes of Empire. It is precisely the heterogeneity of actors who documented their travels in the Age of Exploration and beyond, wherefore a plurality of styles, formats, and discourses proceeds, which renders the task of delineating travel literature extremely challenging. As Van Den Abbeele (1985) remarked at the early stages of postcolonial criticism when "otherness" still proved a "slippery philosophical concept" (p. 5), "the genre of travel literature is, like its subject matter, not easily bounded." But perhaps more important to the (re) construction of history on the basis of travel accounts is the acknowledgment of the quasi-invisible boundary separating fact and fiction, between the real and the fantastic in most of these chronicles.

It takes no less than a towering literary figure from Latin America, a continent "so avidly sought and illusory," to borrow Gabriel García Márquez's (para. 1)[1] words himself, to not only apprehend the fantastical in Pigafetta's account but also to suggest that it "contained the seeds" that would blossom into the mythical Latin American novel where the real and the fantastic seamlessly co-exist (Cachey Jr., 2007: ix). This venture into fantasy of what was intended as a strict record of events is not lost on Filipino literary critic Testa-de Ocampo (2010), who unravelled the "marvelous" in Pigafetta's chronicle alongside other accounts[2] narrating the Magellan expedition:

> Unlike that of Vespucci who stands over a naked America, here Magellan is alone in his ship, the caravel *Trinidad*. The elements of the marvelous

DOI: 10.4324/9781032722320-2

> are there, in the strange lands, peoples and unknown creatures he encounters in the periphery of the engraving. The travel accounts of the Magellan expedition mark the beginning of travel writing on the Philippines with a colonial objective. . . . These surviving foreign accounts are read most of the time for their descriptive value since there are no records left of life prior to the arrival of the Spaniards.
>
> (p. 2)

Just as in Testa-de Ocampo's (2010) literary and political reading of the numerous accounts of the first voyage around the world, Philippine scholarship's engagement with travel writing is predominantly Spanish-oriented. Herein lies the local justification for pursuing this investigation on Italian travel literature set in colonial Philippines. "Italian" observers in the colonial period are much less examined in Philippine historiography compared to their Spanish counterparts. The 300-year Castilian rule over the Archipelago engendered politically engaged scholarship, from the Propaganda Movement (1872–1892), which exposed colonial atrocities through their writings, to contemporary scholars contesting, challenging, and/or demystifying the authority of colonial sources. Thus, archival texts in Spanish and by Spaniards constitute an obvious subject of Philippine scholarly inquiry. Indeed, the inception of Philippine historical research can be traced back to nationalist intellectuals who studied and wrote in Spanish and, "only occasionally, in Tagalog," (Churchill, 2016: 141) the language that would come to be the basis of an independent Philippine national language.

The lack of Filipino scholars proficient in Italian is also a factor, signifying heavy dependence on translation despite the availability of primary sources in the original. From a pragmatic viewpoint, the lesser attention accorded to Italian travel to the Philippines can simply be explained by the smaller number of extant chronicles of Italian origin. Even an up-to-date reader of primary sources on Hispanic incursions into the Asia Pacific unsurprisingly reveals that Spanish-language accounts abound in the transoceanic repertoire,[3] given that Spaniards were the primary agents in conquering and textualising these spaces. Lee and Padrón (2020) accurately observe that the scholarly scrutiny of the "early modern Spanish Pacific" had long been an "exclusive" domain of Philippine studies and only now are we witnessing an emerging dialogue with other disciplines, such as "Latin American studies, Sinology, and Hispanic studies." The scope of this academic interest could thus be expanded by bringing *italianistica* 'Italian studies' into its umbrella of inquiry, not only through the study of primary sources written in Italian or by observers from the Italian peninsula, but also through the acknowledgment of the "Italian" as a distinct subject that at times coincides and at other times conflicts with the "European." For although there have been numerous studies from history, geography, and comparative literature with colonial-era Italian travel writing as the primary material, those who do not specialise in Italian studies often treat the "Italian" chronicler as either an individual, thereby muting the text's specifically "Italian" provenance, or the chronicler is lumped together with the collective "European." In contrast, existing scholarship on travel literature from politically unified Western states who became architects of Empire in the long colonial period displays recognition of a collective discourse of difference that is located in the establishment and fortification of the nation–state. Titles in respectable volumes alone reveal this gap on the Italian subject as an agent of colonial knowledge production given that the Age of Exploration preceded the Italian Unification. For example, *Asian Travel in the Renaissance* includes a study on "The Spanish Contribution to the Ethnology of Asia in the Sixteenth and Seventeenth Centuries" (Rubiés, 2004) and another on "The Far East and the English Imagination, 1600–1720" (Markley, 2004). In contrast, the analysis of Italian texts zeroes in on the individual "Alessandro Valignano: Man, Missionary and Writer" (Ucerler, 2004). Thus, both Philippine studies and the broader field of transoceanic studies could definitely benefit from a thematical and theoretical inclusion of the "Italian's" unique subjectivity.

There are altogether three manuscripts penned by travellers from the Italian peninsula which include descriptions of the Philippine archipelago, its inhabitants, and its customs: Antonio Pigafetta's *Relazione del primo viaggio intorno al globo terracqueo* [Account of the First Voyage Around the Globe][4] (1521),[5] Francesco Carletti's *Ragionamenti del mio viaggio intorno al mondo* [Reflections on my Voyage around the World] (1594), and Giovanni Francesco Gemelli Careri's *Giro del mondo, Vol. V: Le Isole Filippine* [Voyage Round the World, Vol. 5: The Philippine Islands] (1699). Poured over by countless scholars in numerous disciplines, Pigafetta's manuscript bore witness to historical undertakings, such as the first transpacific crossing via what would be known as the Strait of Magellan, a channel linking the Atlantic and the Pacific, and the West's claiming of the Southeast Asian archipelago that would come to be named after the Spanish sovereign, Philip II. His narrative, as opposed to those of his successors Carletti and Gemelli Careri, is thus conferred the unsurpassable rank as the seminal "European" travel to the Philippines. In which he reflects on his 12-year long travel considered to be the first circumnavigation of the globe exclusively for commercial reasons (Pirro, 2021), Carletti's account remains a "major understudied source for global historians" (Riello, 2022). The Florentine merchant's at-times illicit crossing of imperial borders provides insights into the politics of commerce and the intersection of economy and conquest in a radically transformative period. Although said to have sown inspiration for Jules Verne's *Around the World in 80 Days* (1872), a classical work of fictional travel literature (Manzano, 2013), Gemelli Careri's voyage is still "a rather understudied travel report" (Loureiro, 2014: 104) by global and Filipino scholars alike. The Calabrian traveller's intertextual methodology (Loureiro, 2014) of narrating travel while performing ethnography is a valuable resource of contents that were representative of itinerant knowledge production in early modern Europe.

Philippine historiography generally represents a move away from the sixteenth-century humanistic framework that privileged the analysis of aesthetic and rhetorical formalisms over the semiotic creation of entire populations, cultures, and geographies by European chroniclers (Rabasa, 1993: 6). However, the admittedly rare literary analyses of Italian travel (e.g., Mojares, 2002; Testa-de Ocampo, 2010) only deal with Pigafetta by virtue of his testimony's great historical import. Carletti and Gemelli Careri's narrations meanwhile have been insufficiently examined either as primary sources for historical analysis or as literary undertakings. By concurrently surveying all three manuscripts through a combined historical and literary perspective, we break away from the monopolising status of the Pigafetta chronicle in Philippine scholarship as we apply the same analytic rigour to Carletti's and Gemelli Careri's accounts. While these Filipino literary critics and historians account for the literary contexts that shaped Pigafetta's narrative, their strictly postcolonial inquiry ignores the ambivalence of "Italian" travellers as de-territorialised "European" subjects, thus painting travel literature in the Age of Empire with a broad stroke. What, then, lends uniqueness to Italian subjectivity? Despite the prominence of "Italian" travellers in the history and development of maritime discovery (one may effortlessly recall Marco Polo, Christopher Columbus, and Amerigo Vespucci), voyagers from the *Bel Paese* who narrated travel at the height of the so-called Age of Exploration found themselves in a unique position, distinct from that of their European counterparts. As feudal structures began to collapse and with the Papacy's transnational power in steady decline, the Old Continent became a stage for the emergence of nation–states that would become the key players in the colonisation of the New World and the Far East. Italy was not among the grand contenders simply because Italy as a unified political entity would not exist until 1861.

It behooves remembering that the peninsula's arduous march towards the establishment of a unified and centralised state would not commence as a veritable political force until the foundation of *La Giovine Italia* 'Young Italy' in 1831 (Haddock, 1999). In the myth of the Italian nation–state, two figureheads emerged that would come to embody the yin and yang of "thought and action" (Limiti, 2008).[6] Before the more popular Giuseppe (i.e., General Garibaldi) led the *spedizione dei Mille* 'expedition of the thousand' (1860), a military turning point that would unite the Northern and Southern Italian armed forces, Mazzini had formed a nationalist movement after having been driven into exile for spearheading revolutionary activities. In an oft-cited letter to the head of the Savoyard state, Mazzini invoked *La Giovine Italia*'s slogan "*Unione, Libertà, Indipendenza*" 'Unity, Liberty, Independence' embedded on the tricolour banner that would later be adopted as the official national flag of the new centralised state. Signing his letter as "an Italian," Mazzini recognised the unifying potential of King Charles Albert of Sardinia, father of Victor Emanuel II who would be the first to assume the title of King of a unified, independent Italy. Until then, Piedmont had been engaged in geopolitical manoeuvring, expertly swivelling between rival external powers that dominated the Italian peninsula (Montanelli & Cervi, 2013).

> *Sire, respingete l'Austria, lasciate addietro la Francia, stringetevi a lega l'Italia. Ponetevi alla testa della nazione e scrivete sulla vostra bandiera Unione, Libertà, Indipendenza. Dichiaratevi vindice, interprete dei diritti popolari, rigeneratore di tutta l'Italia. Liberatela dai barbari. Edificate l'avvenire. Date il vostro nome ad un secolo. Incominciate un'èra da voi. Siate l'uomo delle generazioni. Siate il Napoleone della libertà italiana.*[7]
>
> (Mazzini, 1831; in Montanelli & Cervi, 2013: 63)

Prior to Mazzini's impassioned call for Italian independence from foreign rule, the travellers Pigafetta, Carletti, and Gemelli Careri ventured away from a peninsula made up of *staterelli*, "the little states of Italy" (Mazzini, 1831; in Stuart, 1919: 35) that enjoyed varying degrees of constitutional and economic sovereignty. Pigafetta and Carletti, originating respectively from the sovereign Venetian and Florentine Republics, and Gemelli Careri, born in the Spanish-ruled Kingdom of Naples, took to travelling and wrote their chronicles within this geopolitical context. Specialists of Italian literature reiterate that the narratives of "Italian" voyagers at the apex of early modern European travel remain underexamined. Inversely, travel to Italy has received more critical attention. The debate was spurred by Cachey (1996) when he foregrounded the "placelessness" at the core of Italian literary identity, followed up by Hester (2003, 2011, 2016), who profoundly investigated the manifestations of the ambiguous "Italian" identity in baroque travel literature. But just as Philippine historiography must broaden its postcolonial range of vision, so can Italian literary scholars benefit from postcolonial thought. Since Cachey (1996) strongly argues for Italian Otherness, he is reticent to interrogate chronicles by "Italian" travellers for their value in imperial episteme. Following in Cachey's footsteps, Hester's (2016) project on the entanglement of travel writing and Italian identity construction dislodges their textual production from "European parameters created by colonial powers that in fact exclude Italians" (23). However, she misses the opportunity to integrate a Bhabhian approach in her investigation of "Italian" ambivalence. It would thus be noteworthy to contribute to existing scholarship on "geographies of belonging" (Mee & Wright, 2009: 772) by foregrounding the unique positionality of "Italian" travellers as they textualised the Philippine islanders.

Manifesting the "disruptive potential" of postcolonial theory, scholars and critics lay bare the structure of representation at the heart of the colonial enterprise "that effectively disordered and jumbled the globe rather than accounted for its differences" (Schmidt, 2015: 22). Within the elaborate descriptions in travel accounts of distant lands and the "curious" peoples that inhabit them are embedded cultural representations that strengthened self-definition while sustaining the legitimacy of colonialism (Castro, 2017). As power and knowledge coalesce, epistemic violence and the legitimisation and naturalisation of rhetorical oppositions take place. Spivak (1988) cites "the remotely orchestrated, far-flung, and heterogeneous project to constitute the colonial subject as Other" (p. 25) as a paradigmatic example of epistemic violence. Meanwhile, the formation of cultural identities, like that of "European," was only possible through the systematic insistence of oppositions (Said, 1994), such as Occident/Orient, Christian/heathen, civilised/uncivilised. This is the core influence of critical theory in travel studies. Proceeding from the Saidian conception of knowledge produced about the Orient by the West as an instrument of fabricating, controlling, and maintaining "a hegemony of power relations" (Burney, 2012: 23), a critical reading of travel unpacks the discursive power contained within and generated by travel accounts. Thus, the discourse of difference transpired through the agency of travel writers.

In pursuit of this line of inquiry, we can investigate how the image of the "Filipino" native is constructed by asking to what extent the "Italian" travellers employ the "rhetoric of othering" (Jasinski, 2001: 412). Are the inhabitants homogenised through a collective appellation or with the use of an "abstracted he/they" (Pratt, 1985: 120)? Are they essentialised with characterisations that "transform social and historical dissimilarities into universal, metaphorical differences" (JanMohamed, 1985: 87)? By addressing these questions, the study can demonstrate how "Italian" chroniclers participated and performed colonial discourse. Indeed, venturing to "far-flung" lands and writing about them constituted an indispensable instrument in advancing the colonial project of knowledge production:

> the persistent importance of ethnographic descriptions as part of a fresh vision of the world in its variety reflected profound anthropological concerns, which greatly influenced the growth of travel narratives as an empirical genre within a wide-ranging experience of colonial expansion.
>
> (Rubiés, 2002: 244)

Yet the inherent relationship between travel writing and postcolonial criticism runs a teleological risk, considering they are "common bedfellows" in a symbiotic relationship whereby the first provides raw materials for analysis to the latter (Lindsay, 2015: 28). For a more refined investigation of the representation of "Filipino" natives in select Italian travel writing, it is imperative to turn our gaze to the travellers themselves. To reiterate the identity-building function of the discourse of difference, "colonial categories for representing the Other were not only constructing an image of the conquerable subaltern but were also fundamental in shaping European identity" (González-Ruibal, 2010: 34). It would thus be formative to consider these travel chroniclers as "subjects" themselves (in the Foucauldian sense). Thus, to nuance "Filipino" Otherness is to scrutinise "Italian" ambivalence. Since cultural identities are inextricably linked with political conditions, it would seem that the Italian travellers under scrutiny had fraught identities as subjects originating from a de-territorialised homeland. Indeed, travel *to* implies travel *away from*.

Postmedieval Italy saw an increased impulse for outward travel among its educated and highly skilled populace due to the lack of an internal political hegemony that could have been instrumental in harnessing its resources. As observed by Italian geopolitics scholar, Manlio Graziano (2010):

> Whatever the cause, the absence of a state, of a central political power capable of offering a national perspective to the wide sweep of the intellectual energies of the peninsula, lay behind the emigration of the most active and gifted of Italians. In order to be able to exercise their talents, the latter found themselves having to put themselves in the service of some foreign power, thus losing all specifically "Italian" character.
>
> (p. 65)

Hence, the most skilful and driven of the populace, many of whom would become indispensable figures in the history of overseas exploration and imperial expansion, diminish or altogether shed any trace of *italitanità* 'Italianness' as they ventured outwards. While Pigafetta sailed under the Spanish Crown, Carletti and Gemelli Careri lacked institutional backing and financed their own ventures. In the process of "losing [their] specifically 'Italian' character" (Graziano, 2010: 65), do these chroniclers accrue a novel identity?

A fundamental component of the experience of travel is the recollection of one's journey. The three Italian chronicles examined here represent a common topos in the Western canon, that of geographic displacement as an avenue for identity building (Monga, 1996: 25). Hence, the writer/traveller makes "use of the familiar to grasp the elusive and unrecognized" (Barth, 1975: 199). The writer's confrontation with the unfamiliar is this study's primary object of analysis, as we will see how the construction of the Other by Pigafetta, Carletti, and Gemelli Careri becomes a tool in the formation of the Self. The voyager's objective is as much the "discovery of his own self" (p. 25) as his quest for learning about the outside world which is attainable only through spatial displacement (Monga, 1996: 25). It is therefore interesting to peer into the discovery of the self through engagement with alterity by de-territorialised subjects not only politically but intellectually speaking. Indeed, the Italian tradition's lack of an original place of provenance from its inception in the Due-Trecento to its high-Renaissance literary consolidation (Cachey, 1996) precluded the establishment of an Italian intellectual centre *à la Parisienne* so that even the foremost thinkers behind the 19th-century *Risorgimento* movement laboured in exile at the heart of the metropole, among the literati of Paris and London. In the second chapter, we will come to see an analogous itinerant operation transpire among the leading proponents of the 19th-century Propaganda Movement that advocated for the consolidation of a *kamayang Pilipino* 'Filipino national consciousness'. To understand how the "Italian" travellers' unique subjectivity is reflected in their writing, we may broadly ask whether their accounts embody the "Italian cultural anxiety about a lack of geographical center and territorial . . .

integrity" (Cachey, 1996: 62). To what extent do they refer to Italy as their provenance? In what contexts do images of Italy, if any, appear, and do these chronicles reflect any detectable "*coscienza di italianità*" 'sense of Italianness' (Croce, 1943: 27)? What must be sought for is the manifestation of an awareness of their ambivalent position as European travellers in colonised domains when the "Italian" subject himself embodied a "European 'other'" (Hester, 2003: 299). It would be a particularly challenging investigation, for the lack of utterance may potentially constitute a signifier, that is, what is eluded could itself carry meaning.

This book thus approaches the body of Italian travel writing to the Philippine Islands through the combined lenses of postcolonial criticism and Italian literary history with particular focus on the geopolitical ambiguity of the "Italian" travel writer. Choosing only one perspective carries limitations, the primary of which is that neither line of inquiry would likely lead to a novel perspective in the critical analysis of travel. This is not to say that either approach could not potentially contribute to existing scholarship. The uniqueness of this cultural crossways alone justifies closer scholarly scrutiny. There are not many historical links bridging the Italian peninsula to the Philippine archipelago, except by way of travel *as journey* and *as text*. It speaks volumes that the "living testament of Filipino-Italian friendship" (Escalante in Saavedra, 2021) is a monument of Pigafetta in Cebu, one of the earliest islands to be converted and conquered by Magellan's crew. Yet a drawback of exclusively employing postcolonial criticism is its self-evident place in travel writing studies. Edwards and Graulund (2011) rightly remark that the reading of travel through a postcolonial lens has, for the most part, addressed only "European(ized) travel" (p. 2), thereby welding the personal act of narrating travel with the political project of building empire:

> In the field of postcolonial studies, travel writing has often been demonized. Critics have, at times, aligned travel narratives with other textual practices associated with colonial expansion – mapping, botany, ethnography, journalism and so on – to suggest that travel writing disseminated discourses of difference that were then used to justify colonial projects.
>
> (p. 2)

Although the present study still deals with travel of European provenance, foregrounding the uniqueness of "Italian" subjectivity nevertheless disrupts notions of "Europeanness" that might appear stable or monolithic in strictly postcolonial readings of travel accounts left by Italian navigators. The same limitation can be said of solely pursuing the matter from a literary historical perspective. It would only serve to confirm, or at best nuance, an already examined feature of the Italian literary tradition. A comprehensive review of these accounts could thus address gaps in the critical reading of travel literature set in colonial Philippines and in the reading of Italian travel literature on the whole. This juxtaposition is called for to fill in the thematic and theoretical lacunae that are observable both in contemporary Philippine scholarly engagement with Italian travel writing and in the analysis of colonial-era travel in the broad field of Italian literary history. This manner of nuancing literary productions by the West while navigating its implications in the East, specifically, as we would come to see in the succeeding chapter, how pre-Unification "Italian" travel informed nationalist constructions in the Revolutionary Philippines, could enrich our understanding of metropole–periphery relations. Only in this manner can we contribute to scholarship serving to "[support] or [critique] the constitution of the Subject as Europe" (Spivak, 1988: 24).

Notes

1 This reference to Pigafetta and the Magellan expedition appears in the opening paragraph of the Colombian writer's Nobel Lecture held on 8 December 1982. In his speech, Gabriel García Márquez erroneously referred to Pigafetta as a "Florentine navigator."

2 Besides Pigafetta's *Relazione*, the only other non-Spanish accounts analysed by Testa-de Ocampo are of the Belgian courtier, Maximilianus Transylvanus' *De Moluccis Insulis* (1524) and Fernando Oliveira's reconstruction in Portuguese of "The Voyage of Fernão de Magalhães to claim the Moluccas for the King of Castile" (1555–1560). The Spanish texts include one of Magellan's mariners, Ginés de Mafra's eyewitness account, the Jesuit missionary Pedro Chirino's *Relacion de las Islas Filipinas* (1604), the Franciscan friar Juan de Plasencia's *Las costumbres de los indios tagalos de Filipinas* (1589), and the Jesuit historian Francisco Colin's *Labor evangélica* (1663).

3 "The 'Spanish Pacific' designates the space Spain colonized or aspired to rule in Asia between 1521, the year Ferdinand Magellan reached the East by sailing west, and 1815, the year when the annual galleon that linked Mexico to the Philippines stopped operating" (Lee & Padrón, 2020: 11).

4 Unless otherwise stated, all translations are my own.

5 The years refer to the start of the voyage to highlight the respective account's place in the historical timeline and so as not to pre-empt the complex publication history of these manuscripts which will form part of the analysis.

6 Garibaldi is often thought to have taken ideological inspiration from Mazzini's writings and activities. For a thorough analysis of the dynamics of the Risorgimento's protagonists, see Limiti's (2008) "Garibaldi and Mazzini: thought and action".

7 "[Sire, repel Austria, leave France behind, unite Italy.] Place yourself at the head of the nation and write on your banner: 'Union, Liberty, Independence.' Proclaim the liberty of thought. Declare yourself the vindicator, the interpreter of popular rights, the regenerator of all Italy. Liberate, her from the barbarians. Build up the future. Give your name to a century; begin a new era from your day" (Stuart, 1919: 34–35).

Reference list

Barth, F. (1975). *Ritual and knowledge among the Bakhtaman of New Guinea*. Yale University Press.

Burney, S. (2012). *Pedagogy of the Other: Edward Said, Postcolonial Theory, and Strategies for Critique. Counterpoints: Studies in the Postmodern Theory of Education. Volume 417*. Peter Lang New York. 29 Broadway 18th Floor, New York, NY 10006.

Cachey, T. J. (1996). An Italian literary history of travel. *Annali d'Italianistica, 14*, 55–64.

Cachey Jr., T. J. (Ed.). (2007). Bio-bibliographical note. In T. J. Cachey, L. Ballerini & M. Ciavolella (Eds.), *First voyage around the world (1519–1522): An account of Magellan's expedition* (pp. xxxvii–lvi). University of Toronto Press.

Castro, M. J. (2017). Tourism and empire: An invitation to colonial travel. Quintana. *Revista de Estudos do Departamento de Historia da Arte, 16*, 225–238.

Churchill, B. R. (2016). Philippine historiography–Looking back and looking forward: The history of historical studies. *Philippine Social Science: Capacities, Directions, and Challenges*, 141–161.

Croce, B. (1943). *Pagine sparse* (Vol. 3). Ricciardi.

Edwards, J. D., & Graulund, R. (Eds.). (2011). *Postcolonial travel writing: Critical explorations*. Palgrave Macmillan.

González-Ruibal, A. (2016). Colonialism and European archaeology. In *Handbook of postcolonial archaeology* (pp. 39–50). Routledge.

Graziano, M. (2010). *The failure of Italian nationhood: the geopolitics of a troubled identity*. Springer.

Haddock, B. (1999). State and nation in Mazzini's political thought. *History of Political Thought, 20*(2), 313–336.

Hester, N. (2003). Geographies of belonging: Italian travel writing and Italian identity in the age of early European tourism. *Annali d'Italianistica. Hodoeporics Revisited/Ritorno all'odeporica, 21*, 287–300.

Hester, N. (2011). Mapping Petrarch in Seventeenth-century Italian Travel Writing. *Humanist Studies & the Digital Age, 1*(1), 128–135.

Hester, N. (2016). *Literature and identity in Italian baroque travel writing*. Routledge.

JanMohamed, A. R. (1985). The economy of Manichean allegory: The function of racial difference in colonialist literature. *Critical Inquiry, 12*(1), 59–87.

Jasinski, J. (2001). *Sourcebook on rhetoric*. Sage Publications.

Lee, C., & Padrón, R. (2020). *The Spanish Pacific, 1521–1815: A reader of primary sources*. Amsterdam University Press.

Limiti, G. (2008). Garibaldi and Mazzini: thought and action. *Journal of Modern Italian Studies, 13*(4), 492–502.

Lindsay, C. (2015). Travel writing and postcolonial studies. In C. Thompson (Ed.), *The Routledge companion to travel writing* (pp. 45–54). Routledge.

Loureiro, R. (2014). Traveling experiences vs. intertextuality. *Anais de História de Além-Mar, 15*, 101–136.

Manzano, D. (2013). Gemelli and his travel to the Philippines. *Asian Perspectives in the Arts and Humanities, 3*(1), 101–122.

Markley, R. (2004). Riches, power, trade and religion: The Far East and the English imagination, 1600–1720. In D. Carey (Ed.), *Asian travel in the Renaissance*. Blackwell Publishing.

Márquez, G. G. (1982, December 8). The solitude of Latin America. *The Nobel Prize*. www.nobelprize.org/prizes/literature/1982/marquez/lecture/

Mee, K., & Wright, S. (2009). Geographies of belonging: Why belonging? Why geography? *Environment and Planning: Economy and Space*, *41*(4), 772–779.

Mills, S. (2003). *Discourses of difference: An analysis of women's travel writing and colonialism*. Routledge.

Mojares, R. B. (2002). *Waiting for mariang makiling: Essays in philippine cultural history*. Ateneo University Press.

Monga, L. (1996). Travel and travel writing: An historical overview of hodoeporics. *Annali d'italianistica*, *14*, 6–54.

Montanelli, I., & Cervi, M. (2013). *L'Italia del Risorgimento-1831–1861*. Bur.

Pirro, D. (2021, July 14). Francesco carletti. *The Florentine*. www.theflorentine.net/2021/07/14/italian-sketches-francesco-carletti/

Pratt, M. L. (1985). Scratches on the face of the country; Or, what Mr. Barrow saw in the land of the bushmen. *Critical Inquiry*, *12*(1), 119–143.

Rabasa, J. (1993). *Inventing America: Spanish historiography and the formation of Eurocentrism* (Vol. 11). University of Oklahoma Press.

Riello, G. (2022). Carletti's world: An early modern global voyage. *European University Institute*. www.eui.eu/DepartmentsAndCentres/HistoryAndCivilization/ResearchAndTeaching/ResearchProjects/Carletti-world-an-early-modern-global-voyage

Rubiés, J. P. (2002). Travel writing and ethnography. In P. D. Hulme (Ed.), *The Cambridge companion to travel writing* (pp. 242–260). Cambridge University Press.

Rubiés, J. P. (2004). The Spanish contribution to the ethnology of Asia in the sixteenth and seventeenth centuries. In D. Carey (Ed.), *Asian travel in the renaissance*. Blackwell Publishing.

Saavedra, J. R. (2021, April 14). HCP turns over refurbished Pigafetta statue to Cebu City. *Philippine News Agency*. www.pna.gov.ph/articles/1136687

Said, E. (1994). *Culture and imperialism*. Vintage.

Schmidt, B. (2015). *Inventing exoticism: Geography, globalism, and Europe's early modern world*. University of Pennsylvania Press.

Spivak, G. C. (1988). Can the subaltern Speak? In C. Nelson & L. Grossberg (Eds.), *Marxism and the interpretation of culture*. University of Illinois Press.

Stuart, E. M. (1919). Modern Italy and her struggle for liberty. *Fine Arts Journal*, *37*(3), 30–39. https://doi.org/10.2307/25587627.

Testa-de Ocampo, A. M. (2010). The marvelous turn in the accounts of the Magellan expedition to the Philippines in the 16th century. *Journal of English Studies and Comparative Literature*, *10*(1).

Ucerler, M. A. J. (2004). Alessandro valignano: Man, missionary and writer. In D. Carey (Ed.), *Asian travel in the renaissance*. Blackwell Publishing.

Van Den Abbeele, G. Y. (1985). Introduction. *L'Esprit Créateur*, *25*(3), 5–7. www.jstor.org/stable/26284375

2 The place of travel writing in the mapping of national discourse

Although Dante's infernal peregrination is the most cited case of symbolic travel in the Western medieval canon, travel has failed to make a resounding echo in the formation of the Italian literary canon (Cardona, 1986: 687). Only in recent years have we witnessed increasing attention to *hodoeporics* among Italian literary critics, most notably Cachey's (1996) seminal essay sketching "(a)n italian literary history of travel," Polezzi's *Translating Travel: Contemporary Italian Travel Writing in English Translation* (2017), Hester's *Literature and identity in Italian baroque travel writing* (2016). All these studies highlight the tumultuous dynamics of travel writing, a genre that is in itself complex and has often escaped a strictly bounded definition, within the Italian literary system. Cachey's (1996) epistemological study of travel across Italian literary history reveals travel writing as "a marginal literature or a 'historical' genre" (p. 57), while Hester (2016) explains that the lack of critical attention accorded to travelogues of Italian origin, especially those written in the early modern period, is a function of the genre's "tentative status" in world literature and, more precisely, travel writing's rather "problematic" locus in the Italian milieu where it has "[historically] occupied non-literary categories" (p. 11). Polezzi (2001) succinctly notes the "double absence" (p. 1) that is the hitherto inexistent tradition of critical scrutiny of Italian travel and the scarcity of travel writing produced by Italians in contrast with the abundance of travel literature produced about Italy.

The very denomination "Italian travel writing" is ambiguous. Any nuanced investigation of travel within the Italian context must consider that the Italian tradition of narrating European voyage co-existed with the reality of Italy as a European destination (Polezzi, 2017). Most strikingly, the Grand Tour during the Age of Enlightenment popularised the ritual of upper-class Europeans experiencing and representing "Italy as a site for discovery, a bridge to Antiquity, and a path to pleasurable exotic adventure" (Hester, 2016: 4). As we will come to see, subjectivising the Italian traveller reveals the ambivalent discourse engendered by documenting one's engagement with the foreign. This ambivalence stands out in contexts where "foreignness" and "otherness" are not fixed but are rather unstable categories that represent "shifting

DOI: 10.4324/9781032722320-3

positionalities" (Bhabha, 1994: 70). The binary opposition of the Self and the Other, which is a salient feature of colonial discourse, is dislodged from its fixity when we consider "Italian" Otherness within early modern European constellations, a condition that is rooted in pre-Unification Italy's subjugation to European colonial powers (De Donno & Srivastava, 2006: 375). The intellectual configurations that shaped a historically fragmented and nascent Italy nestled in geopolitical ambivalence indeed prove an interesting semiotic resource for emancipatory constructions in the periphery:

> Italy's radical and nationalist traditions, which have had such an evident influence on anti-colonial and postcolonial thought, can perhaps be linked to the peculiarities of Italy's historical evolution as a nation and its ambiguous position as regards Europe and modern European colonialism. A primary ambivalence is given by the fact that the pre-unification Italian states had been colonies of various European empires before united Italy became a European colonial power itself.
>
> (De Donno & Srivastava, 2006: 375)

Travel *to* (not *away from*) has been subject to wider and closer scrutiny in Italian scholarship. For instance, the volume *L'Italia dei grandi viaggiatori* 'The Italy of Great Travellers' (Paloscia, 1986) talks not of the Italian peninsula that birthed historic globetrotters. Written from within, it centres, rather, on the rhetorical construction of "Italy" by literary giants who travelled across the peninsula, the likes of Gogol, Mark Twain, Henry James, and Goethe. For many Italian scholars, it is imperative to probe European representations and semiotic creations of Italy before the unified nation space was carved out. Locating the nation in textual production comes as no surprise if we recall the words of Italian poet, Giosuè Carducci. The Nobel Prize laureate and elected senator of the Kingdom of Italy (1890) challenged his country's designation as a mere "geographical expression" by invoking the nascent political entity's historical literariness:

> *A Metternich, che aveva definito l'Italia "un'espressione geografica", Carducci replicava che l'Italia è piuttosto "un'espressione letteraria", riproponendo una delle idee forti che avevano accompagnato il processo risorgimentale, cioè che l'Italia, sebbene non fosse mai esistita politicamente, era già presente nella coscienza dei letterati fin dal tempo di Dante. La storia della letteratura italiana si è configurata perciò fin dalle origini come una vera e propria storia d'Italia, spesso la sola (gloriosa) possibile.*[1]
>
> (Jossa, 2006: 2)

Yet the articulation of Italy as a literary expression had not been the exclusive domain of the peninsula's literary forefathers (that is, the poetic triumvirate of Dante, Boccaccio, and Petraraca) and the generations of Italian writers to succeed them. Equally valuable as primary materials for the critical reading of "*l'Italia letteraria*" 'literary Italy' (Jossa, 2006), an alternative or, some may argue, prerequisite to "*l'Italia nazione*"[2] 'the nation Italy' (Turtulici, 2022: 218) are travel narrations about Italy by external observers.

In her book *Italianità: la costruzione del carattere nazionale* 'Italianness: constructing the national character,' Patriarca's (2010) analysis of the ongoing formulation and negotiation of a national consciousness is interspersed with references to exogenous depictions of Italy and Italians. The cultural historian even offers a bibliographic footnote of scholarly work on how Europeans, through a varied typology of texts,[3] perceived and constituted the Italian as "Europe's historical internal Other" (Nathan, 2017: 52) throughout the modern period. The peculiarity, or rather, ambivalence (as many Italian studies scholars would put it) of "Italian Otherness" lies in its proximity to the beholder of the gaze – the European. Past the mid-eighteenth century, with the Grand Tour in full swing, an interesting account emerged written by a literary émigré from Turin, known among the English literati as Joseph Baretti (1769). Himself a prolific narrator of travel within Europe,[4] Baretti (1769) wrote an ethnographical treatise of his own country where he sought to redress the gaps in exogenous representations about the peninsula and its inhabitants. With special focus on English travellers, Baretti interpreted European "allegations" of Italian moral ineptitude as misinterpretations of local culture by tourists who ignored the language and approached their target destination superficially (Patriarca, 2010: 48). In his work aptly titled *An Account of the Manners and Customs of Italy with Observations on the Mistakes of some Travellers with Regards to that Country*, he warns and defends his *patria* of the essentialising rhetoric of travelogues which, as we would see in the final chapter, was also a ubiquitous facet of Italian travel writing about colonial Philippines. Baretti's (1769) professed motivation for producing a countertext to European travel to Italy was "to caution [the generality of travel writers] against being too ready to condemn everything but what they have seen practised at home," and reads almost like an admonition to the exoticisation of native customs by foreign observers. The European tourists who roamed and wrote about the Italian peninsula were criticised for "[travelling] to see things, and not men" (p. 372) Even so, no tour, regardless of the "superficiality" of its motive, precludes contact with another populace. The identity of the Self emanates from engagement with the Other in the way that Frenchmen touring Italy in the early modern period gained self-perception through contact with the Italian *Autre* (Bideaux, 1996: 90): "*le séjour en Italie permet au Français de la fin du XVI*ᵉ *siècle d'affirmer au contact de cet Autre sa perception de sa propre identité*"[5] (p. 94). Bideaux's (1996) reading of French travel to Italy will be revisited in the fifth chapter as a juxtaposition to our reading of Italian travel to the Philippine Islands.

While European travel writing about Italy discloses the Italian subject's ambivalence in continental discourse, scholarly work betrays the equally ambiguous place occupied by travel in Italian literary history. In fact, seminal works often overlook the genre of travel and omit it from their categorical analyses. Cachey (1996) makes the astute observation that the canon's lack of a special category for travel is partly due to its ubiquity in the Italian literary universe where themes of exile and/or pilgrimage form the narrative base.

> For the Italian tradition, both at its origins in the Due-Trecento, and at the time of its consolidation during the high Renaissance, did not emerge from any one center but rather represented the creation, by a dispersed intellectual class, of a literary and linguistic ideal which was sought, pursued, and was present potentially in every geographical Italian center or locale, but original to none of them. Dante describes it as "the panther we are stalking" in the *De vulgari eloquentia* (I, xvi), "that animal who scatters its fragrance everywhere and shows itself nowhere." Accordingly, Italian literature has from its founding "exiles," Dante and Petrarch, established itself as a tradition seeking to overcome its lack of an original place, either to depart from, or to which return.
>
> (Cachey, 1996: 55–56)

In gross terms, Father Dante himself was a chronicler. The quintessential *Divina Commedia* is effectively an account of the poet's "*viaggio nei tre regni dell'Oltretomba*" 'journey through the three kingdoms of Beyond' (Asor Rosa, 2009a: 370). Yet despite recognising travel as a recurrent element in Italy's narrative tradition (Asor Rosa, 2009b: 267), even an authoritative volume approaching Italian literary history from a European perspective allots a mere four-pager on the textual production of explorers. Not in contemporary scholarship and not even during their most prolific period, when Italian chronicles were circulated and read voraciously throughout Europe, did travel reach the status of high literature (Vittorini, 2017: 7). The value of Italian travel writing should hence be sought elsewhere, precisely where it served rather than betrayed a purpose. That place is Europe. Analysing Italian travel writing to the Middle East, Vittorini (2017: 7) confidently speaks of the European canon as a welcome host for Italian chroniclers. The volume *Rereading Travellers to the East: Shaping Identities and Building the Nation in Post-unification Italy* provides a fresh and much-needed merging of Italian travel studies and a strand of Saidian criticism that actively departs from a "monolithic portrait of the orientalizing West" (Falcucci et al., 2022: 16). They argue that Italian narrations of Oriental geographies, produced from the embryonic stage of the Kingdom of Italy to the summit of Fascist Italy's colonial venture, constituted a necessary building block of a post-Unification national glory at the core of which loomed the disgrace of Italy's historically fragmented Self:

> While the post-unification Italian actors that we discuss were almost always part of the dominant classes, their discourses about "Italian" travellers were often framed in revanchist terms, thus betraying the profound inferiority complex of the new Italian elite: against the more solid national

> narratives, not to mention the stronger economies, fully-fledged academic traditions and larger colonial empires of other European countries such as the United Kingdom, France and Germany, the Italian actors struggled to move from a position of perceived inferiority and historical dispossession to the place in the world that Italy allegedly deserved.
>
> (Falcucci et al., 2022: 11)

While travel towards Italy subjected its inhabitants to European gaze, travel away from Italy exposed the peninsula's de-territorialised and fragmented nature. The latter revealed the regional (rather than national) attachments of the "Italians" venturing out. Thus, the unstable coordinates of travel writing as a genre within the Italian literary system can be honed in by navigating the thorny intersection between geopolitics and cultural formation. The lack of any "specifically 'Italian' character" (Graziano, 2010: 65) in itinerant textual production was thought to betray the canon's "fundamental trajectory and inspiration" which, taking cue from the European political zeitgeist, idealised "territorial definition and linguistic integrity" (Cachey, 1996: 56).

Travel writing by Italian explorers is at once regional, when viewed from within pre-Unification Italy, and cosmopolitan, when viewed from without by early modern Europe. Curiously, Asor Rosa (2009b) only parenthetically mentions this peculiar feature as he remarked how cosmopolitan intellectuals broadened the ideological compass of the "*civiltà italiana (in quel momento soprattutto civiltà regionale, e solo dopo europea)*" 'Italian civilsation (at the moment, mostly regional civilsation, and then only later European)' (pp. 267–268). Could this be a literary scholar's cautionary measure for invoking an anachronistic Italian civilisation without contradicting the national literary ideal? Nonetheless, the Italian explorers' cultivated cosmopolitan character (Asor, 2009a: 499) drove them to leap from the regional straight to the continental, diffusing European ideals whilst bypassing the formation of the Italian national character (Patriarca, 2010). The exportability of Italian intellect thus rendered the peninsula's navigators valuable to Europe's enterprise of knowledge at a time when knowledge became a legitimising force for the Old Continent's violent and disruptive material ventures. Gramsci (1996) invites us to rethink travel writing by Italians beyond the framework of proto-Italian nationhood. Rather than seek the "national" element of Columbus' "discovery" of America, he historicises Italian intellectual development through its international European function (Gramsci, 1996: 161).

> *La nascita di Cristoforo Colombo in un punto dell'Europa piuttosto che in un altro ha un valore episodico e casuale, poiché egli stesso non si sentiva legato a uno Stato italiano. La quistione, secondo me, dovrebbe essere definita storicamente fissando che l'Italia ebbe per molti secoli una funzione internazionale-europea. Gli intellettuali e gli specialisti italiani erano cosmopoliti e non italiani, non nazionali. Uomini di Stato, capitani,*

> *ammiragli, scienziati, navigatori italiani non avevano un carattere nazionale ma cosmopolita. Non so perché questo debba diminuire la loro grandezza o menomare la storia italiana, che è stata quello che è stata, e non la fantasia dei poeti o la retorica dei declamatori: avere una funzione europea, ecco il carattere del "genio" italiano dal '400 alla Rivoluzione francese.*[6]

Hester (2016) warns against uniformly attributing Italian cosmopolitanism to the "seamless adoption" (p. 22) of a European identity that was, in itself, undergoing formation. But if we regard as valid the observation that "Europe did not simply expand overseas [but also] made itself through that expansion" (Asad, 2002: 220), then the Italian subject who was an authorial agent during the Age of Exploration, and whose narrative fell in line with the rhetorical and semiotic conventions of that epoch's expansionist project, can be said to have performed European identity through the language of colonial discourse. We must take the opportunity here to highlight the action word "to perform" in lieu of Hester's (2016) "to adopt." In the fifth chapter, we will witness the semiotic creation of the "Filipino" natives by the "Italian" voyagers who fell into the trap of exoticism and essentialisation, mechanisms of meaning-making that Baretti (1769) decried about European travellers to Italy. As Bhabha (1996) affirms, "terms of cultural engagement, whether antagonistic or affiliative, are produced performatively" (p. 2). Cachey (1996) outright discourages judging Italian travel writing "according to the standard of hegemonic trends of European colonial writing" (p. 23) on the basis of Italian Otherness. While we echo Cachey's (1996) and Hester's (2016) calls to challenge Saidian essentialism by highlighting the "Italian" subject as a counterhegemonic figure, to ignore Italian travel writing's dialectical relationship with colonial discourse would be an equally limiting vision of Italian subjectivity. Bhabha (1994) cautions that, "the taking up of any one position, within a specific discursive form, in a particular historical conjuncture, is thus always problematic – the site of both fixity and fantasy" (p. 77). To understand the novel and critical value in reading the fraught Italian subjectivity against the itinerant "Italian" intellectual's participation in the formation of colonial epistemes prior to Italy's political Unification and subsequent attempts at empire building, let us shift our gaze to cosmopolitan intellectuals from the extreme periphery.

As Italy was facing turbulent times in efforts to stabilise the peninsula into a unified territory, anticolonial sentiments were brewing in the late eighteenth-century Philippines. The archipelago was an insular colony whose management depended heavily on religious orders and whose material importance was limited to maritime trade via the Manila–Acapulco galleon (Schumacher, 1973). Dating back to the earliest contact between Magellan's crew and the islanders, the three-century Castilian rule had sown seeds of discontent that would sprout into a reformist movement and a revolutionary struggle. Any separatist revolt from a power perceived to be foreign must first proceed from the consciousness of a like-minded community, a nation so to speak, even if it is a "fluctuating [entity] that people are just giving shape to" (Fanon, 1969; in Bhabha, 1994: 152). Gramsci (1996) postulates that a national trajectory cannot be sketched by single subjects, but by a collective's conscious and organic expression of a "*blocco sociale nazionale*"[7] 'national social bloc' (p. 154). Philippine historiography generally credits national formation to two distinct campaigns which the prevailing narrative bisects along social and class cleavages (Justiniano, 2016). On one hand, the Propaganda Movement (1880–1896) was constituted by the Filipino intelligentsia, designated as the upper-class "*ilustrados*" 'enlightened ones.' On the other hand, the *Kataastaasan, Kagalanggalangang Katipunan ng mga Anak ng Bayan (Katipunan)* 'Supreme and Honorable Association of the Children of the Nation' was a popular organisation founded in 1892 that plotted an armed uprising to overthrow colonial authority. Our sublimation of travel writing as a semiotic resource for the formulation of a national consciousness in the Philippine context is hinged upon the first, since it is in the intellectual movement of the Philippines' itinerant nationalists where travel (as *journey* and as *text*) once again proves instrumental.

The last operational galleon was named after the first European navigator to cast anchor at a Philippine island. In 1811, this Spanish sailing vessel transported the last batch of precious cargo such as porcelain, spices, silk, ivory, and a host of other exotic commodities from Manila to Acapulco. Unlike its Portuguese namesake, *Magallanes* managed to return to its port of origin four years after it had set sail, "[bringing] to an end an epoch of maritime history" (Dillon, 1951: 123). The erosion of the galleon's commercial monopoly in the Spanish East Indies catalysed trade in the region and rendered the port of Manila ever more accessible to foreign merchants (Borlaza). The opening of the Suez Canal under French auspices in 1869 heralded transformations in maritime politics and commerce, tipping the balance in favour of Great Britain while thwarting "the hopes of the Mediterranean nations" that a quicker route equalled greater economic prosperity (Fletcher, 1958: 564). Beyond the commercial drawbacks it spelled for the Spanish Crown, the Suez Canal also brought about radical social transformations in the only Spanish colony in the Asia Pacific. Slashing travel time from five months to only one, this new route increased the influx of *peninsulares* (born in Spain and of pure Spanish descent)[8] to the archipelago, increasing the number of Spaniards fivefold.[9] It also made westward travel accessible to an admittedly privileged segment of the colonial Philippine populace. The cosmopolitan Filipino is thus born.

The rise of a Filipino middle class came as a result of growth in commercial agriculture while the archipelago's opening to international trade (Dela Goza & Cavanna, 1985) bred a generation of Filipinos with the means and impulse to venture to the metropole. While outbound travel in the service of Europe designated the locus for a proto-national Italian identity according to Gramsci, outbound travel towards Europe (then still under the haze of libertarian, egalitarian, and fraternising ideals) sparked the beginning of a Philippine independentist movement according to Mabini. In his political and ideological treatise called *La revolución filipina* (written between 1864–1903), Mabini reflects on the intimate link between the opening of the Suez Canal and the formation of a veritable "*blocco sociale nazionale*" 'national social bloc' to borrow from Gramscian lexicon:

> *La revolución política de Filipinas es de origen reciente: puede decirse que su formación empezó solamente desde la apertura del Canal de Suez, inaugurada en noviembre de 1869. Los anteriores levantamientos habían sido motivados por agravios inferidos a una localidad o a determinadas personas, y no por la necesidad de reformas políticas generalmente sentida; razón por cual no pasan de simples motines.*
>
> (Mabini, 1931: 278)

Conferred the title of "*utak ng himagsikan*" 'brain of the Revolution' in popular history, Apolinario Mabini y Maranan was only one among a select group of scholars, mostly mestizos[10] from well-off families, who would be regarded as the ideological forefathers of the Filipino nation.

Travelling to the West to harness itinerant knowledge, they would form a new intellectual and social class with the double aim of unveiling Spanish atrocities to their fellow Filipinos and dialoguing with the Crown to gain political representation. The first was to be achieved by morally educating the Filipino people to value liberal ideals (Schumacher, 1973), the second by making Spain cognizant of its colony's needs while dispelling racist tropes and contesting colonialist rhetoric (Manalo, 2022). Here, travel as *journey* emerges as a prerequisite to nation-building while travel as *text* became a valuable resource for counter-knowledge production. As we flesh out Philippine scholarly engagement with Italian travel writing in the fourth chapter, we will come to understand how the "transformation of the *indio* into a Filipino" (Majul, 1973: 28) rested upon the Propaganda Movement's appropriation and subversion of Western representations of the Philippine Islands and its inhabitants as they figured in travel narratives.

In Philippine historiographic orthodoxy, these itinerant, Western-educated propagandists occupy an ambivalent position. Except for the mythical figure of national hero, José Rizal,[11] the propagandists were largely dismissed by historians as launching a "futile 'reform movement'" (Schumacher, 1973: xviii). Their amphibious character – travelling back and forth between periphery and centre, shifting between indigenous and Western epistemologies – did not fit into the unitary nationalist mould of indigenous historiography (Claudio, 2013; Justiniano, 2016). In the same vein, outbound explorers like Pigafetta, Carletti, and Gemelli Careri transgressed the heavy industry of Italian nationhood anchored on the European mythology of the monolithic nation–state, since their narrations unmasked "an original lack of geographical center, territorial definition, and integrity" (Cachey, 1996: 56). Developments in postcolonial criticism have led to new methodological considerations in historicising the nation (Sethi, 2005). In recent Philippine scholarship, there has been a shift towards valorising the "brains of the nation" (Mojares, 2006) despite and because of their engagement with international worldviews. Much like how Gramsci (1996) interpreted cosmopolitanism as integral to Italian intellectual history, Filipino historians revisit the intellectual foundations of the Philippine Revolution that had been set in motion by the transmarine movements of its foremost proponents. Instead of simply treating national consciousness as organically produced, in slight defiance of Gramscian terms (see previous quote [1996: 154]), Mojares (2006) and Thomas (2012) place emphasis on the agency of colonial subjects in modern knowledge production. A contrapuntal reading of the Filipino intellectual movement in the late nineteenth century disrupts the coloniser–colonised binary by highlighting the deployment of Western thought in service of imagining and constructing the pre- and postcolonial nation.

> [T]he biographies of these figures reveal the surprising connections and creations possible among those who travel between and among peripheries and centers . . . [locating] an origin of Filipino nationalism in the Filipino intelligentsia's ambivalent relationship to . . . Castilian-Spanish worlds.
>
> (Thomas, 2012: 15)

This take on *ilustrado* cosmopolitanism effectively dislodges Filipino historical figures from fixed nationalist discourses, employing a Bhabian outlook on the formation of national consciousness by locating the nation in the liminal.

By and large, highly educated "Italians" and "Filipinos" voluntarily crossed geographic, cultural, and intellectual borders. Our reading foregrounds how the Italian chronicler, documenting their travels in the Age of Exploration, represents a shifting positionality that fluctuates between being Othered and Othering. We argue that he does so by venturing away from a fragmented homeland of "chronic ambivalence" (Nathan, 2017: 51) to territories ripe for or submitted to conquest. Far from his native terrain, he takes part in the production of "fantasmatic knowledges [which] construct the positionalities and oppositionalities of racist discourse" (Bhabha, 1994: 95). Centuries later, at the waning of the Spanish Empire, these cosmopolitan Italians' narratives would be unearthed by cosmopolitan Filipinos ceasing histor(iograph)y in their own hands. Indeed, the *ilustrados* did not only travel; perhaps more importantly, they studied travel. From the standpoint of contemporary Philippine scholarship, travel away from the periphery towards the metropole by native cosmopolitans and travel away from the metropole towards the periphery by foreign explorers need both be subject to critical elaboration. Encountering chronicles about the Philippine Islands in European archives, the propagandists challenged Western epistemological authority on Filipino ontology. In sum, their travel to the West allowed these cosmopolitan *ilustrados* to become "the first 'natives' in Southeast Asia to engage Orientalist scholarship in its homegrounds" (Mojares, 2006: 503–504). Before delving deeper into Philippine intellectual engagement with the Italian travel writing in the fourth chapter, it is first necessary to contextualise the Italian chroniclers' narratives by interrogating each one's motives for travel.

Notes

1 "To Metternich, who had defined Italy as 'a geographical expression', Carducci replied that Italy is rather 'a literary expression', reintroducing one of the strong ideas that had accompanied the Unification process; the idea being that Italy, although it had never existed politically, was already present in the consciousness of the literati since Dante's time. The history of Italian literature has, since its inception, therefore been configured as a true history of Italy, often the only (glorious) one possible."

2 We can add Turulici's (2022: 218) observation to the numerous analyses by contemporary Italian scholars of the fledgling national consciousness in the immediate aftermath of the birth of the Kingdom of Italy: "*L'idea, la coscienza di costituire una nazione erano patrimonio solo delle élites di nobili e borghesi che avevano attivamente partecipato al processo di unità politica. La più gran parte delle popolazioni della penisola e delle isole del paese non aveva, non poteva avere nessuna idea di cosa fosse l'Italia nazione. Era italiana solo sulla carta*" ['The idea, the consciousness of constructing a nation, were the exclusive heritage of the elite, the nobility, and the bourgeoisie who had actively participated in the process of political unification. The vast majority of the population did not, could not have any idea of what constituted the nation Italy. Italy was only a nation on the map.'].

3 In her footnote, Patriarca (2010) introduces these texts thus: "*Per una trattazione esauriente di come gli europei vedevano e descrivevano l'Italia e gli italiani in una varietà di scritti – dispacci diplomatici, resoconti di viaggio, libri di storia – dalla fine del XVII alla metà del XIX secolo*" ['For a comprehensive treatise on how Europeans perceived and described Italy and the Italians in a variety of texts – diplomatic dispatches, travel accounts, history books from the end of the seventeenth century to the mid-nineteenth century.'].

4 For an autobiographical and bibliographic portrait of Baretti, see Mühlschlegel's (2011) "*De paisajes y palabras: Joseph Baretti, viajero y lexicógrafo*" 'Of landscapes and words: Joseph Baretti, traveller and lexicographer.'

5 "Travel to Italy during the 16th century allowed the Frenchman to affirm his perception of his own identity through contact with that Other."

6 "The birth of Christopher Columbus in a certain part of Europe rather than another has no value other than as a matter of chance since he himself did not feel linked to an Italian state. The question, in my opinion, should be posed historically by establishing that Italy had, for many centuries, an international-European function. Italian intellectuals and experts were

cosmopolitan and not Italian, not national. Italian statesmen, captains, admirals, scientists, and navigators did not have a national but a cosmopolitan character. I don't know why this should diminish their greatness or undermine Italian history, which has been what it has been and not that imagined by poets or declaimed by orators: having a European function, that's the trait of Italian 'genius' from the 1400s to the French Revolution."

7 Gramsci's (1996) formulation of nationhood is exclusively situated in the engineering of a collective with a shared awareness: "*l'influsso storico di una nazione non può essere misurato dall'intervento individuale di singoli, ma dal fatto che questi singoli esprimono consapevolmente e organicamente un blocco sociale nazionale*" 'a nation's historical influx cannot be measured on the basis of the individual intervention of a select few, but on the fact that these individuals express, consciously and organically, a national social bloc' (p. 154).

8 This ethno-social designation in the colonial Philippine caste system is distinct from the *insulares*, full-blooded Spaniards born in the Philippines.

9 We are given these estimate figures: "By 1870, there were about 13,500 Spaniards (including creoles), while in 1810 there had been only some 3,500 to 4,000. These foreigners brought social and governmental ideals of the 19th century European and American Liberalism."

10 The term was an ethnic designation for Filipinos with a mixed descent and is usually associated to a high social standing because of miscegenation with Spaniards.

11 José Rizal (1861–1896) is a revered intellectual and nationalist figure in Philippine history. Author of the novels *Noli me tangere* (1887) and *El filibusterismo* (1891), his "subversive" writings were thought of to inspire the *Katipunan* to armed revolt. He was executed by the colonial government in 1896.

Reference list

Asad, T. (2002). Muslims and European identity: Can Europe represent Islam? In A. Pagden (Ed.), *The idea of Europe: From antiquity to the European union* (pp. 209–227). Woodrow Wilson Center Press.

Asor Rosa, A. (2009a). *Storia europea della letteratura italiana I. Le origini e il Rinascimento*. Einaudi.

Asor Rosa, A. (2009b). *Storia europea della letteratura italiana II. Dalla decadenza al Risorgimento*. Einaudi.

Baretti, G. (1769). *An account of the manners and customs of Italy: With observations on the mistakes of some travellers, with regard to that country* (Vol. 2). Nabu Press.

Bhabha, H. (1994). *The location of culture*. Routledge.

Bideaux, M. (1996). Le Voyage d'Italie, instrument de la connaissance de soi par la fréquentation d'autrui. *Annali d'Italianistica*, *14*, 89–102.

Cachey, T. J. (1996). An Italian literary history of travel. *Annali d'Italianistica*, *14*, 55–64.

Cardona, G. (1986). I viaggi e le scoperte. In A. Asor Rosa (Ed.), *Letteratura Italiana: Le questioni* (Vol. V, pp. 687–716). Einaudi.

Claudio, L. E. (2013). Postcolonial fissures and the contingent nation an anti-nationalist critique of Philippine historiography. *Philippine Studies: Historical and Ethnographic Viewpoints*, *61*(1), 45–75.

Croce, B. (1943). *Pagine sparse* (Vol. 3). Ricciardi.

De Donno, F., & Srivastava, N. (2006). Colonial and postcolonial Italy. *Interventions: International Journal of Postcolonial Studies*, *8*(3), 371–379.

Dela Goza, R. S., & Cavanna, J. M. (1985). *Vincentians in the philippines 1862–1982.* Congregacion de la Mision en Filipinas, Inc.

Dillon, R. H. (1951). The last plan to seize the Manila Galleon. *Pacific Historical Review*, 20(2), 123–125.

Falcucci, B., Giusti, E., & Trentacoste, D. (2022). New Perspectives on Nation-building and Orientalism in Italy from the Risorgimento to the Republic. In *Rereading Travellers to the East Shaping Identities and Building the Nation in Post-unification Italy* (pp. 9–28). Firenze University Press.

Fletcher, M. E. (1958). The Suez Canal and world shipping, 1869–1914. *The Journal of Economic History*, *18*(4), 556–573.

Gramsci, A. (1996). *Gli intellettuali e l'organizzazione della cultura.* Editori Riuniti.

Graziano, M. (2010). *The failure of Italian nationhood: The geopolitics of a troubled identity.* Springer.

Hester, N. (2016). *Literature and identity in Italian baroque travel writing.* Routledge.

Jossa, S. (2006). *L'Italia letteraria.* Mulino.

Justiniano, M. C. S. (2016). Reviewed works: "Brains of the nation: Pedro Paterno, T. H. Pardo de Tavera, Isabelo de los Reyes, and the production of modern knowledge" by Resil B. Mojares; "Orientalists, propagandists, and ilustrados: Filipino scholarship and the end of Spanish colonialism" by Megan C. Thomas. *The Journal of Asian Studies*, *75*(2), 556–559.

Mabini, A. (1931). *La revolución filipina (con otros documentos de la época)* (Tomo 2). Bureau of Printing. www.cervantesvirtual.com/obra/la-revolucion-filipina-con-otros-documentos-de-la-epoca/

Majul, C. A. (1973). *The relevance of Mabini's social ideas to our times.* https://www.asj.upd.edu.ph/index.php/archive/121-vol-11-no-1-april-1973

Manalo, A. R. (2022). Ilustrado, revolutionaries or accomplices of the Spanish Empire: The contested influence of Filipino ilustrados on Philippine National Independence (1872–1898). *Synergy*. https://utsynergyjournal.org/2022/02/06/ilustrado-revolutionaries-or-accomplices-of-the-spanish-empire-the-contestedinfluence-of-filipino-ilustrados-on-philippine-national-independence-1872–1898/

Mojares, R. B. (2006). *Brains of the nation: Pedro Paterno, TH Pardo de Tavera, Isabelo de los Reyes, and the production of modern knowledge.* Ateneo University Press.

Nathan, V. (2017). *Marvelous Bodies: Italy's New Migrant Cinema* (Vol. 70). Purdue University Press.

Paloscia, F. (Ed.). (1986). *L'Italia dei grandi viaggiatori*. Edizioni Abete.

Patriarca, S. (2010). *Italianità: la costruzione del carattere nazionale*. Gius. Laterza & Figli.

Polezzi, L. (2017). *Translating travel: Contemporary Italian travel writing in English translation*. Routledge.

Schumacher, J. N. (1973). *The propaganda movement, 1880–1895: The creators of a Filipino consciousness, the makers of revolution*. Solidaridad Publishing House.

Sethi, R. (2005). New Frontiers of Transcultural Space: Problematizing Identity and Nation. *Indian Literature, 49*(6 (230)), 137–149. http://www.jstor.org/stable/23346306

Thomas, M. C. (2012). *Orientalists, propagandists, and ilustrados: Filipino scholarship and the end of Spanish colonialism*. University of Minnesota Press.

Turtulici, S. (2022). *Giovanni Giolitti. Liberale una specie perduta*. LAReditore.

Vittorini, V. (Ed.). (2017). *Il viaggio in Oriente – Antologia dei resoconti dei viaggiatori italiani nel mondo arabo nel XIX secolo*. Giorgio Pozzi Editore.

3 The "Italian" chroniclers' motives for travel

What political historians designate as the Early Modern Period coincides with what geographical historians define as the Age of Exploration. The impetus that drove innumerable men to undertake lengthy, perilous expeditions was manifest fully in Europe during the "long sixteenth century" (Chase Dunn, 2012). But travel towards remote, hitherto unknown territories was not a novel phenomenon; travellers had set out eastwards away from the Italian peninsula as early as the thirteenth century. However, travel did assume a different meaning as Europe transitioned to Modernity. This era of unprecedented mobility was at once the catalyst and the consequence of innovations in transportation technology. The praxis of travel was facilitated as geographic coordinate systems were updated, cartographic studies were commissioned, new land and maritime routes were established, and an entire industry on the "art of travel" came into being (Cambi, 2011: 154). Meanwhile, the very conception of travel itself was reinvented. The "long sixteenth century" was a period that irrevocably changed the world system through a trinitarian structure of power with intersecting sociocultural, economic, and political dimensions, ushering a new era of understanding and interpreting the world, conducting commercial affairs, and engineering societies (Wallerstein, 2004: 21). While the Church wielded its political power to back expeditions, travel itself was "revolutionised" in its abstract dimension.

> *Con la Modernità, quindi, la fisionomia del viaggio . . . assume valori nuovi – di conoscenza, di socializzazione, di formazione – in una società che si fa sempre più cosmopolitica; si dispone anche come sfida e come avventura, animato dalle tensioni dell'ignoto, della scoperta, etc.; si fa metafora, oltre che mezzo, della formazione del soggetto e, insieme, del rinnovamento della visione della società).*[1]
>
> (Cambi, 2011: 154)

In an emerging cosmopolis, travel presented itself as both a limitation to overcome and an unmissable undertaking to Europe's educated class. As such, humanist philosophy was enriched by an expanding intellectual "horizon

DOI: 10.4324/9781032722320-4

resulting from travel" (Szönyi, 2018: 5). This conceptualisation of travel took root in renaissance philosophy that saw the collocation of man, rather than God, at the centre of being. The human condition was thus reconceptualised by reconfiguring the role of the individual. Shackling the restrictive reins of medieval philosophy, the individual regains his capacity to mould himself and his own destiny even as he assumes the responsibility to concretise that potential. The Renaissance man must then confront the responsibility to make sense of his own being by understanding the material conditions wherein he is immersed. As such, he is encouraged to venture beyond the familiar, towards the foreign, driven by the desire to aggrandise his own vision of the world (Hale, 1983: 136). From the medieval conception of travel as transcendence, whose central theme was the pursuit of God, the reparation of sins, and the attainment of Christian justice (Cambi, 2011), the modern formulation of travel transformed it into self-discovery through confrontation with alterity (Monga, 1996).

No wonder then did the early modern period behold a wealth in the publication of theoretical treatises to instruct the curious humanist on how to conduct travel, how to observe while travelling, and how to document one's experiences and reflections (Szönyi, 2018: 14) in service of expanding humanist thought through "the combination of philology, historical interest, and the proposition of new ideas" derived from the act of travelling (Szönyi, 2018: 5). Cambi (2011) traces the genesis of Modernism to a twofold reformulation of the signifier "travel" that reveals a stark parallelism in the subjectivisation of Europe as *the* continent and of the European as *the* individual:

> *Il primo è un viaggio che rimescola le carte culturali dell'Europa e la allontana dalla sua condizione medievale e cristiana. Il secondo ne rinnova il baricentro, la fisionomia, legando il viaggio al soggetto, all'individuo e ri-qualificandolo come sua propria esperienza e/o avventura. Sul primo fronte si collocano i viaggi di scoperta (e di conquista) come pure, in relazione al puro immaginario, i viaggi in utopia, in quel "paese che non c'è" ma che è necessario attraversare e attraversare con l'immaginazione. Sul secondo, invece, si dispongono i viaggi di formazione (di cui il Grand Tour sarà l'interprete e il modellol).*[2]
>
> (p. 154)

It is precisely this modern redefinition of travel which situates it in the infrastructure of knowledge that lays bare the ambivalence of the "Italian" subject. On the one hand, Italian travellers, whether religious or secular, held chief importance in the "discovery" of the New World and the subsequent rewriting of the globe as a lasting consequence of European exploration-cum-conquest. On the other hand, Italy's position as a European "tourist" destination in the *Grand Tour* rendered Italians as textualised subjects themselves who figured in their imperial neighbours' travel narrations and their attendant ethnographic descriptions. Europe's Age of Discovery engendered a self-image that was no longer merely inherited from ancient traditions but is begotten out of contrastive encounters with others, transforming the Old Continent from "a peripheral frontier of ancient centres" (Leed, 1991: 160) to "a center in its own right and a culmination of history on the cutting edge of the 'modern'" (p. 21). More precisely, it is the "religious arrogance" (Mancall, 1998: 28) of designating a previously populated region as terra nullius that marked Europe's "discovery" of its modern Self in the wake of a New World.

> "To sucke out some profit," as Acosta put it, was the goal of the Europeans, as is evident in extant historical writings, but historical writing has another aim: history became a tool which Europeans used to integrate an outpouring new information into already existing mental universes. . . . Europeans had to learn how to observe the territory entered; how to describe what they saw for others to read; how to disseminate those texts within Europe; and most difficult of all . . . how to comprehend what those texts meant.
>
> (Mancall, 1998: 37)

We must again take not of the subjectivity of Western travellers like Pigafetta, Carletti, and Gemerlli Careri in an era where travel's function as a self-didactic resource for the individual (Monga, 1996: 19) went hand in hand with its intrumentalisation for empire-building by continental powers (Leed, 1991: 159). The enhancement of the individual's intellectual compass is thus intimately bound with the continent's geographical expansion.

While sojourning in Barcelona under the sponsorship of the papal nuncio, Francesco Chiericati (1479–1539), Antonio Pigafetta heard news of an expedition to set sail from Seville towards the Moluccas (Perocco, 2015). While little is known of Pigafetta's life before his Spanish sojourn, we know from his writings that he studied with the humanist philosopher Pietro Pomponazzi (1462–1525). Neither a marine nor a geographer, but bearing a strong papal recommendation, the young Vicentino was appointed as "*criado del capitán y sobresaliente*" 'the captain's right-hand man and *sobresaliente*' (Aguinagalde, 2019: 202). The *sobresaliente*'s duty was restricted to defending the fleet in case a battle ensued, and this title was reserved to men who joined either for love of adventure or for military ambitions (Jal, 1848: 1410). He boarded the flagship Trinidad of the five-ship fleet led by Portuguese navigator Ferdinand Magellan. The *Relazione*[3] opens with Pigafetta's (1956) dedication to his patron, Philippe de Villiers de L'Isle-Adam, which he concludes by citing the chief motive for his travel:

> *avendo io avuto gran notizia per molti libri letti e per diverse persone, che praticavano con sua signoria, de le grandi e stupende cose del mare Oceano,*

> *deliberai, con bona grazia de la maestà cesarea e del prefato signor mio, far esperienzia di me e andare a vedere quelle cose, che potessero dare alcuna satisfazione a me medesimo e potessero partorirme qualche nome appresso la posterità.*[4]
>
> (p. 7–8)

Consistent the humanist habitus (Aguinagalde, 2019: 202), the chronicler confirms his zeal as neither militarily nor politically driven, but arising from a personal mission to enrich his vision of the world and earn prominence in the process. As previously mentioned, Renaissance thinking reconceptualised "man" as a subject confronted with the challenge to construct his own destiny through the acquisition of knowledge about the Self and, by extension, the World. This process of self-actualisation necessarily involves geographic displacement. Travel abroad was consequently envisioned as a necessary phase in the constitution of the "*honneste homme*," a cultivated being expected to maximise one's faculties (Monga, 1996: 19).

Unlike his antecedent who had sailed on a Spanish-funded voyage, or his successor who would independently travel away from a Spanish holding, Carletti set sail as a self-financed merchant from a *patria* that occupied a valuable position in the global arena. Highlighting Tuscany's role in the age of empire, Brege (2021: 325) observed how Carletti's testimonies detailing a universe of natural resources, "exotic" practices, and commercial networks were a prized resource for the Medici, who had a profound understanding of the economic and political advantages of this emerging global infrastructure of knowledge. Fondly designated as the world's first tourist, Carletti travelled and traded for nearly a decade (1594–1602) from the West to the East Indies and back (De Filippi, 1931). His initial destination was Cape Verde, where he intended to "*comprare delli schiavi neri per portarli all'Indie occidentali et quivi venderli*" 'acquire black slaves to bring to the West Indies and sell them there' (Carletti, 1958: 8). The 18-year-old departed from Florence to the thriving cosmopolis of Seville where Pigafetta had boarded the Magellan fleet towards the East Indies. After two years of working closely with a fellow Florentine trader, Carletti was joined by his father, Antonio, who had secured an illicit agreement to acquire permission for his son's voyage (Marcocci, 2020: 334). Father and son ventured out in January 1594 after successfully circumventing Spanish directives. By "abusing the malleability of identity and family ties" and taking advantage of "shadow commerce" (Brege, 2021: 124), these Tuscan merchants, working outside the parameters of empire as private traders from a "*staterello*" 'small state,' accessed lands, seas, and resources otherwise unreachable to those who were not legal subjects of Empire. After cruising through Panama, Mexico, Colombia, and Peru, he returned to Acapulco, which was connected to the Philippine Islands via the Manila Galleon. From there, he sailed to Japan and then China, before passing through Malacca,

Ceylon, and Portuguese India on his way back to the Old Continent. There, he would step on Dutch and then French soil before his return to Florence.

Driven by the possibility of commercial profit, Carletti set himself apart from Pigafetta and Gemelli Careri, whose express aims were, respectively, the prospect of posterity and the likelihood of literary distinction. Typical of the genre's conventions, the *Relazione*'s and the *Giro*'s dedications not just named their patrons but also the voyage's "*raison d'être*" (Motsch, 2011: 214). This, however, is omitted from the *Ragionamenti*'s[5] dedication:

> *L'aver io, Serenissimo Prencipe, insieme con li mia beni di fortuna, perso anche tutte le mie scritture e memorie, ch'io avevo fatto delli viaggi conseguiti da me nel circondare tutto il mondo, sarà causa ch'io non potrò cosi minutamente raccontare a V. A. ogni particularità di quanto ho visto et aveva osservato e notato ne' suddetti mia scritti; de' quali non mi rimane altro, che una poca di memoria travagliata dalle miserie occorsemi: la quale al meglio che mi sarà possibile vedrò di riscorrere e d'andarmi rammemorando solo di quelle cose che ho fatte e viste in detti mia viaggi, e d'ogn'altro mio successo, fino ad essere ritornato in questa città di Firenze alla presenza di Vostra Altezza Serenissima questo di 12 di luglio 1606.*[6]
>
> (Carletti, 1958: 7)

Rather than elucidate the rationale of his odyssey, Carletti turned his patron's attention to his receding memory and misfortunes, for which the author made recourse to previous chronicles during writing. As we will see in their bibliographic history, Gemelli Careri, travelling and writing more than a century later, would employ the same intertextual reliance on extant literature (Loureiro, 2014) in his reconstruction of his travels and in his quasi-encyclopaedic mode of representing native customs.

To circumnavigate the world was not part of Gemelli Careri's initial plan; his original itinerary only included the Holy Land and the Chinese Empire. Unlike Pigafetta, who mostly engaged in scholarly pursuits, or Carletti, who was exclusively profit-driven, Gemelli Careri had a military background which was put to full use in the 1686 Battle of Buda fought between the Holy League and the Ottoman Turks. His military service earned him high praises from the Hapsburgs, who, as a form of gratitude, helped reinstate him in the Neapolitan judiciary, albeit for a limited time. He enjoyed this comfortable post for two biannual terms, after which he decided to embark on the journey that would bring the *Giro* to life (Doria, 2000). Most available literature on the life of Gemelli Careri paints him as a man of adventure (Doria, 2000). Even before disembarking from Naples in 1698, his trips to Europe's cultural hubs (i.e., Venice, Paris, London, Amsterdam, Cologne, and Vienna) at the age of 35 attest to his "cultivated attitude regarding the art of travel" (Loureiro, 2014: 104). Gemelli Careri left Naples in June 1698, and visited Egypt, Jerusalem, Constantinople, Armenia, Persia, India, China, and Manila. From the Far East, he crossed the Pacific, saw Mexico and then voyaged to Spain, proceeded to southern France, and finally returned to the Italian *Mezzogiorno* or southern Italy. He would re-enter Naples via the West Indies fleet after his five-year odyssey. Although it is still uncertain how the traveller financed his own enterprise, what remains irrefutable is the lack of any apparent political, religious, or commercial motive underpinning his travel. Gemelli Careri's decision to invest and embark on an autonomous voyage with the scant means at his disposal was in itself a curious feat and earned him the praise of his contemporaries (Magnaghi, 1932).

In contrast with Pigafetta's courtly roots, Gemelli Careri's bourgeois rather than noble origins had gatekept him from his epoch's literati. The Calabrian's motive for documenting his voyage brings the *questione della lingua* 'the language question' to the fore. Despite originating from the Kingdom of Naples, Gemelli Careri's body of work was written "*in stil Toscano*," that is, in the language and style of literary Tuscan. It must be noted that Pietro Bembo's seminal work, *Prose della volgar lingua* (1595), catapulted Tuscan into a vehicle for the "highest form of literary expression" (Hester, 2016: 33). Pigafetta's text, dated before this defining moment of codification that would set forth linguistic prescriptions to travel writers (Hester 2016), was written in a "bizarre Italo-Venetian language with Spanish words mixed in" (Magnaghi, 1935). Unlike his Calabrian successor, the Vicentino's quest for personal glory was not framed in literary terms. On the contrary, Gemelli Careri's stylistic allegiance to the towering figure of Petrarch (Hester, 2016) and his decision to write in the literary lingua franca may have been manifestations of his pursuit of that "*onorato luogo nella Reppublica Letteraria*" 'honorary place in the Literary Republic' (Gemelli Careri, 1719: 287 in Buccini, 1996: 255). Unlike the commercially, religiously, and politically motivated travels that dominated European press at the time (Loureiro, 2014: 129), Gemelli Careri's *Giro*[7] emerged from the author's desire to acquire prominence as a travel writer with all the perceived advantages of such a social standing. Carletti's use of Tuscan, by contrast, was not a conscious decision but rather a simple consequence of his hailing from a culturally and linguistically prominent *patria*.

As summed up by Hester (2016), "the *questione della lingua* remains an essential backdrop of Italian travel writing and its relationship to shifts in identity-building during the early modern period" (p. 52). The distinct historical and political configurations in which the three Italian chronicles emerged, as manifest in their diverging linguistic and rhetorical qualities, would also play a role in the publication of each travelogue. In the following chapter, pertinent details shall be provided on each text's bibliographic history, exhibiting how the (re)production of travel as text can be as arduous as travel itself as journey. This will be accompanied by a discussion of Philippine scholarly engagement with Italian travel writing.

Notes

1 "Thus, with Modernity the physiognomy of travel . . . assumed novel values – of knowledge, of socialiation, of formation – in a society that was becoming cosmopolitan, travel at once became a challenge and an adventure, enlivened by the tensions of the unknown, by discovery, etc. It grew into a *metaphor* of, apart from being a means of, forming the individual subject alongside transforming society's vision."

2 "The first is a journey that shuffled Europe's cultural cards and distanced it from its previous medieval, Christian condition. The second adjusted Europe's centre of gravity, its physiognomy, linking travel to the individual subject and re-defining it as the individual's own experience and/or adventure. The first is exemplified by voyages of discovery (and of conquer) as well as travel in relation to the imagination, such as travels to Utopia, to the 'land that is not there' but that which must be crossed by means of imagination. The second, on the other hand, is exemplified by educational travels (for which the Grand Tour served as a model)."

3 For convenience, Pigafetta's chronicle will henceforth be referred to as the *Relazione*. All direct quotes in the original derive from the Ambrosiana manuscript (1800) as it appeared in the 1956 edition of the *Relazione del primo viaggio intorno al mondo* edited by Camilo Manfroni and published by Istituto Editoriale Italiano.

4 "[H]aving learned many things from many books that I had read, as well as from various persons, who discussed the great and marvelous things of the Ocean Sea with his Lordship, I determined, by the good favor of his Cæsarean Majesty, and of his Lordship abovesaid, to experience and to go to see those things for myself, so that I might be able thereby to satisfy myself somewhat, and so that I might be able to gain some renown for later posterity" (Pigafetta, 2007: x).

5 For convenience, Carletti's chronicle will henceforth be referred to as the *Ragionamenti*. All direct quotes in the original derive from the 1958 edition published by Giulio Einaudi editore.

6 The fact, Most Serene Prince, that I lost, along with my worldly goods, all my writings and memoranda about the voyages I made while going around the world will explain why I shall not be able to recount to Your Highness in minute detail all the particulars of what I had seen and observed and had noted in the abovementioned writings. Nothing of them remains to me but a few memories, and they afflicted by the miseries I underwent. I shall try to the best of my ability to go over them again and to remember only those things which I did and saw in my abovementioned voyages and all the things that befell me until I was back in the city of Florence in Your Serene Highness's presence on this day, July 12, 1606 (Carletti, 1964: 7).

7 For convenience, Gemelli Careri's chronicle will henceforth be referred to as the *Giro*. All direct quotes in the original derive from the 1700 edition published in Naples by Giuseppe Roselli.

Reference list

Aguinagalde, F. B. (2019). Habent sua fata libelli. Elcano y la construcción del relato de la primera circunnavegación, una historia apasionante de errores e imprecisiones. *Anais de Historia de Alem-Mar*, *20*, 173–214.
Brege, B. (2021). *Tuscany in the age of empire*. Harvard University Press.
Buccini, S. (1996). Coerenza metodologica nel "Giro del mondo" di Giovanni Francesco Gemelli Careri. *Annali d'Italianistica*, *14*, 246–256.
Cambi, F. (2011). Il viaggio come esperienza di formazione. Tra diacronia e sincronia. Studi sulla Formazione. *Open Journal of Education*, *14*(2), 149–171.
Carletti, F. (1958). *Ragionamenti del mio viaggio al mondo*. Giulio Einaudi Editore.
Carletti, F. (1964). *My voyage around the world* (H. Weinstock, Trans.). Pantheon Books.
Chase-Dunn, C. (2012). The emergence of predominant capitalism: The long sixteenth century. *Contemporary Sociology: A Journal of Reviews*, *41*(1), 9–12.
De Filippi, F. (1931). Carletti, Francesco. *Enciclopedia Italiana Treccani*. www.treccani.it/enciclopedia/francesco-carletti_%28Enciclopedia-Italiana%29/
Doria, P. (2000). Gemelli Careri, Giovanni Franesco. *Enciclopedia Treccani: Dizionario Biografico degli Italiani* (Vol. 53). www.treccani.it/enciclopedia/gemelli-careri-giovanni-francesco (Dizionario-Biografico)/
Gemelli Careri, F.G., *Giro del mondo*, Venezia, Giovanni Malachini, 1719.
Hale, J. R. (1983). Gunpowder and the renaissance: An essay in the history of ideas. *From the Renaissance to the Counter-Reformation*, 113–44.
Hester, N. (2016). *Literature and identity in Italian baroque travel writing*. Routledge.
Jal, A. (1848). *Glossaire nautique* (Vol. 3). Firmin Didot frères.
Leed, E. J. (1991). *The mind of the traveller. From Gilgamesh to global tourism*. Basic Books.
Loureiro, R. (2014). Traveling experiences vs. intertextuality. *Anais de História de Além-Mar*, *15*, 101–136.
Magnaghi, A. (1935). Pigafetta, Antonio. *Enciclopedia Italiana Treccani*. https://www.treccani.it/enciclopedia/gemelli-careri-giovanni-francesco_(Enciclopedia-Italiana)/
Mancall, P. C. (1998). The age of discovery. *Reviews in American History*, 26(1), 26–53.
Marcocci, G. (2020). Mobility, global interaction and cultural transfers in the age of exploration. In A. Arcangeli, J. Rogge & H. Salmi (Eds.), *The Routledge companion to cultural history in the Western world* (pp. 331–347). Routledge.
Monga, L. (1996). Travel and Travel Writing: An Historical Overview of Hodoeporics. *Annali d'italianistica*, *14*, 6–54.

Motsch, A. (2011). Relations of travel: Itinerary of a practice. *Renaissance and Reformation/Renaissance et Réforme*, *34*(1–2), 207–236.

Nectoux, F. (2001). Nationalism and culture: some reflections on the construction of national languages. STROINSKA, M.(éd.), *Relative Points of View: Linguisitic Representation of Culture*, New York & Oxford: Berghahn Books, 81–98.

Perocco, D. (2015). Pigafetta, Antonio. *Enciclopedia Treccani: Dizionario Biografico degli Italiani* (Vol. 83). www.treccani.it/enciclopedia/antonio-pigafetta_(Dizionario-Biografico)

Pigafetta, A. (1956). Relazione del primo viaggio intorno al mondo. In C. Manfroni (Ed.), *Collana Viaggi Esplorazioni Scoperte*. Istituto editoriale italiano.

Szönyi, G. E. (2018). Broadening horizons of renaissance humanism from the antiquity to the new world. *Primerjalna književnost*, *41*(2).

Wallerstein, I. (2004). *World-systems analysis: An introduction*. Duke University Press.

4 The "Italian" chronicles' journey towards publication

When Pigafetta returned to the Old Continent in 1522 aboard the Spanish carrack *Victoria*, he brought with him a much sought-after document. It was his personal journal, which he had painstakingly written throughout the three-year expedition. The story of the first recorded successful attempt to circumnavigate the globe was an object of extreme fascination among European nobility for its tremendous intellectual and political implications. The author, who was among the only eighteen survivors of the 265-man crew that comprised the Magellan–Elcano expedition, was warmly received in the wealthiest courts of Europe. Among his audience were the Renaissance art patron, Isabella d'Este, her husband, Giovan Francesco II Gonzaga (Marquis of Mantua), Pope Clemens VII (a Medici), and Philippe de Villiers de L'Isle-Adam, the knight to whom the account had been dedicated (Vagnon, 2010). To this day, his narrative remains a curious object of study for its singular historic value and has been extensively analysed by scholars from its time of publication to the present (McCarl, 2019). At its inception, the *Relazione* was a compendium of summaries of writings en route that the navigator would weave into a full manuscript in 1524 (McCarl, 2019: 86). The preserved manuscripts reflect the version of the text dedicated to Philippe de Villiers de l'Isle Adam, most likely due to the voyager's close ties with the Knights of Rhodes (Vagnon, 2010). There are four extant codices, three of which were published in French, and all include 23 coloured maps drawn by the chronicler (Cachey, Jr.: xlvi). The earliest is the unpublished MS fr. 24.224, followed by the MS. fr. 5650, published in Paris in 1525 and currently housed in France's Bibliothèque Nationale. The latter, bearing the title "*Premier voyage autour du monde/par le chev. Pigafetta; sur l'escadre de Magellan, pendant les années 1519, 20, 21 et 22; suivi de l'extrait sur le chevalier Martin Behaim ; avec la description de son globe terrestre; orné de cartes et de figures*,"[1] formed the basis for all succeeding editions before the nineteenth century (Vagnon, 2010: 86). Last among the French manuscripts was the Phillips MS 16405, popularly known as the Yale Codex, which is stored in the Beinecke Rare Book and Manuscript Library. The Ambrosiana codex is the only manuscript in Italian and is considered the most representative of the original language employed

DOI: 10.4324/9781032722320-5

by the chronicler. It is also deemed the most complete among the four extant codices. Transcribed by Augustinian encyclopaedist Carlo Amoretti and published in Milan in 1800, this codex was especially significant as it dispelled all doubts regarding the language used by Pigafetta in documenting his travels.[2]

Amoretti's transcript was the famed Ambrosiana codex chanced upon at the British Museum by José Rizal, one of the major proponents of the intellectual and reformist Propaganda Movement (1880–1898). This occurred during his second sojourn in Europe, where the Filipino nationalist devoured literary and historical texts about the Philippine Islands. His scholarly mission to annotate one of the earliest first-hand accounts of the Spanish colonial venture in the Pacific, Antonio de Morga's *Sucesos de las Islas Filipinas* (1609), led him to several other sources of great interest. Mojares notes (2002: 55) the situational irony in which the Philippine national hero then found himself. The colonised subject, journeying in the "fogbound heart of empire," where he discovered a document detailing the "discovery" of his homeland by its would-be colonisers, denoted a crucial moment in the (re)writing of Philippine history. Rizal (1889) enthusiastically wrote about his textual discovery to his fellow propagandists, stressing the urgency of translating the chronicle into either language of the Propaganda Movement (Spanish or Tagalog).

> Haga V. que uno de los de allí aprenda el italiano porque yo tengo aquí manuscritos italianos que tratan de la primera venida de los españoles a Filipinas: están escritos por un compañero de Magallanes, y como no tengo tiempo para traducirlos por mis muchos quehaceres, bueno sería que un paisano los traduzca al tagalo o castellano para que se sepa cómo estábamos en 1520. El italiano es fácil, en un mes se aprende con el Método de Ahn. Ahora estoy aprendiendo el holandés.[3]
>
> (Rizal, 1889: 297)

Pigafetta's testimony represented a point of departure to argue that an indigenous civilisation existed before European intercourse. By translating the text, the Filipino intelligentsia could hark back to an identity that was untainted by European textual production, even if these nationalists found themselves relying on Western textual production to revitalise their sense of "Malayness" as a precolonial origin of identity (Mojares, 2013: 214). This "uncontaminated" space would have set the stage for the genesis of a nationalist mode of writing (about) history.

It bears repeating that Rizal and his contemporaries constituted the earliest collective engagement in peripheral Southeast Asia with Orientalist scholarship of Western provenance (Mojares, 2006). The Propaganda Movement's intellectual and political endeavours, embodied by the mythical Rizal, made a resounding echo in colonial Southeast Asia as a clear-cut case of the subaltern toiling to break through the inherited muteness. As a thinker operating from what Spivak (1988: 78) delineates as the "margins (one may call the silent, silenced center," Rizal's intellectual and methodological legacy in the Southeast Asian postcolonial imaginary is manifest in Malaysian scholar Shaharuddin bin Maaruf's book, *Concept of a Hero in Malay Society* (1984), where the Filipino propagandist figures among "three ideal heroes to emulate" (Nery, 2011: 44), and in Indonesian national hero Tan Malaka's philosophical treatise *Madilog: Materialisme, Dialektika, Logika* (1943), where Rizal, alongside the Filipino proletarian revolutionary Andres Bonifacio, are represented as figures that "play a significant role in raising the Indonesian people from the inferiority complex caused by European colonialism" (Tan Malaka [1943] in Guillermo 2017: 343). A reframing of his people's past, Rizal envisioned, provided the necessary intellectual groundwork for the formulation of a national consciousness from within, and the Pigafetta chronicle represented precisely that opportunity. Indeed, the traveller's first-hand account of precolonial landscapes and customs still serves as a semiotic resource for nativist depictions of the Philippines that invoke that original Malayness, elusive though it may seem. This is articulated by award-winning Filipino filmmaker, Lav Diaz, who exhibits visual nostalgia of a precolonial Filipino identity rooted in Malay stillness as deference to nature:

> I always think of nature as Malay, but . . . there is a very imposing Catholic perspective as well. The creation or the imagination of Filipino culture is a mix of Catholicism and Malay influences. In trying today to think of this Malay past, there is no written record; the only reference is to the tribes of Mindanao. Perhaps the only written record is the diary of Antonio Pigafetta [an observational diary, written in Italian when the explorer was aboard Ferdinand Magellan's ship]. . . . And for a culture that has no written record, it's a great document. The narcissism of Magellan and his desire to have everything chronicled became a source of historical value. It's my only reference to the Malay ways during that period before the Spanish arrived.
>
> (Guha & Diaz, 2020: 22)

Seen in this light, the propagandists' commitment in forging a counter-discourse to hegemonic epistemology could be read as a unique instance of "decolonial" thinking in the Southeast Asian region even before the disruption of formal colonial relations and as an instrument to morally and politically justify native calls for independence. It can thus be said that Rizal's textual encounter with Pigafetta in 1889 had set the tone for the role that the latter's narrative would play in Philippine historiography.

The very same manuscript "discovered" by Rizal would be published two decades later, during the early years of American colonisation of the Philippines. A transcript of the Ambrosiana codex was reproduced by American historians in the colossal volume, *The Philippine Islands* (1902), where they compiled primary sources pertinent to the Philippines spanning three centuries (1493–1898). They pinned the beginning of the archipelago's documentary history on the demarcation conflict between Spain and Portugal that culminated in the historic signing of the Treaty of Tordesillas (1494), which partitioned the post-Columbian world between the two great powers:

> for out of [these two powers] grew Magellan's voyage and the discovery of the islands; and without them the Philippines would no doubt have been occupied by Portugal and later have fallen a prey to the Dutch as did the Moluccas. (Bourne, 1902: 19)

The denouement of Blair and Robertson's (1902) documentary endeavour is pinned on the year of Spain's cession of the Islands to the Americans, signalling that "the old régime in the Philippines has disappeared forever" – that is, the colonial venture which subjected the indigenes to "a life which was so remote from the outside contemporary world that they might as well have been living in the middle ages in some sheltered nook . . . entirely oblivious of the progress of knowledge" (p. 19). Underneath this open derision of Spanish colonial legacy by American historians lay the tautological "altruistic aims" of the new colonial administration (Cano, 2008: 4). Just as the Spanish colonial enterprise stood on an infrastructure of knowledge, so did American academia constitute a cog in the imperial machinery. Despite covering a relatively early period of Philippine documentary history, Pigafetta's narrative came out in Blair and Robertson's Volumes XXXIII and XXXIV, rather than in Volume II where it chronologically fit. This is because the editors undertook to provide an exact transcription of Pigafetta's chronicle, along with an English translation, since it had "never hitherto been adequately presented to the world" (Blair & Robertson, 1902: 89). This rendered Pigafetta accessible to Filipino scholars who were not conversant in either Italian or French, simultaneously conferring to it an authoritative status as a first-hand account and exposing it to the scrutiny of a people eager to retell its own history, the discursive construction of which had previously been monopolised by its conquerors. The English translation thus resulted in abundant academic examination of the *Relazione*.

Towards the end of the sixteenth century, Carletti's function as merchant and reputation as the first traveller to circumnavigate the globe through public means of transport accorded him the status of a descendant of Marco Polo. Even before the trader's return to Florence, he had already been invited to Paris to recount his tales to Henry IV (Sgrilli, 1906: 457). Beyond his personal interests, Carletti's testimony offered itself up to a diverse set of disciplines and proved of great interest not just to politicians and statesmen, but also to "anthropologists, historians of ideas, art historians, economists" (Monga, 1996: 48). The period following his homecoming in 1606 witnessed a prolific collaboration between the merchant/traveller and the Medici family that persisted even after the Grand Duke Ferdinand's death. Alongside the textual reconstruction of his odyssey, Carletti also wrote a trader's treatise, *Relazioni di viaggi e negozi che si fanno per tutte le Indie* 'Accounts of voyages and business around the Indies.' The manuscripts comprising the *Ragionamenti* would not be printed until 1701, already sixty-five years after the author's demise. We owe this textual debut to the bibliographic and editorial work of Lorenzo Magalotti, who decided to publish the completed account posthumously (Dei, 1987: 22). The manuscript bore the title *Ragionamenti di F.C. fiorentino sopra le cose da lui vedute ne' suoi viaggi, sì dell'Indie Occidentali, e Orientali come d'altri Paesi.*[4] Only two centuries later would this first edition be subject to scrutiny. Sgrilli's (1906) biobibliographical monograph revealed the inconsistencies, censorship, and personal liberties that Magalotti had taken with the original manuscripts (p. 250). To date, it is believed that the manuscript closest to the original is the Codex 1331 (T.3.22), which is the oldest extant version preserved in the Biblioteca Angelica of Rome (Dei, 1987: 22; Colla, 2008: 114). This codex formed the basis of the 1958 edition, edited by Gianfranco Silvestre and printed by Giulo Einaudi Editore. Despite the value of his travels as an epistemological resource, his reconstructed testimony has decidedly fewer editions and reprints than Pigafetta's or Gemelli Careri's.[5]

Whereas Pigafetta was ensured a grand European audience for the seminal implications of the first circumnavigation of the globe and Carletti was warmly welcomed in the Medici court thanks to "Florence's global outlook" (Brege, 2021: 1), Gemelli Careri did not immediately come into renown as a narrator of travel. His first two literary attempts, the *Viaggi per l'Europa* 'Travels Around Europe' (1693) and the *Relazione delle campagne d'Ungheria* 'Account of the Hungarian Campaigns' (1698) went scarcely noticed (Doria, 2000). It was thanks to his *Giro del mondo*, comprised of six volumes that were originally published in Naples between 1699 and 1670, that the author/adventurer was consigned to the literary map of his epoch. This was the last and solely successful of three publications under his name. The initial destination of Gemelli Careri's voyage was the Ottoman domain, while the last leg of his trip was through the New World. These diverse locations bookended his voyage, resulting in a literary enterprise spanning what is now designated as the Middle East (*Vol. I: Turchia, Vol. II: Persia, Vol. III: Indostan*), the Far East (*Vol. IV: Cina, Vol. V: Le Isole Filippine*), and the Hispanic Americas (*Vol. VI: Nuova Spagna*). The *Giro* immediately gained widespread attention not limited to Neapolitan intellectual circles (Buccini, 1996). Writing in literary Tuscan guaranteed him readership throughout the peninsula. Seven Italian editions came out between the first year of its publication and 1728. This recognition was certainly not confined within the Italian peninsula, but soon extended throughout the rest of Western Europe. The initial publication of Gemelli Careri's voyage was followed by several translations into the principal European languages of his time while excerpts of his six-volume account were published in various European periodicals, one of which was English, four French, one German, and another Russian (Doria, 2000).

The historical and literary value of his manuscripts is best understood when they are regarded as "founding documents of a literature of globalisation on pure whim" (Sloterdijk, 2013: 38). Indeed, the "touristic" function of Gemelli Careri's odyssey positions his chronicles within modernity's textual and cultural repertoire. Despite, or perhaps because of, the author's innovative adventure, the publication of the *Giro* triggered countless criticisms that sought to invalidate not just the accuracy of the account but the veracity of the voyage itself. One such accusation suggested that Gemelli Careri had succumbed to illness before having had the chance to set out on a journey and was too incapacitated to even move out of Naples. The author was further accused of inventing "facts" and of having made recourse to plagiarism by copying statements and descriptions from previous travelogues (Loureiro, 2014). His critiques adopted the humanist habitus as these denunciations were grounded on early modern epistemology's "growing demand for authenticity" (Szönyi, 2018: 14). Nowadays, the veracity of his actual journey is no longer contested thanks to authoritative eyewitness accounts by scholars and fellow explorers, such as the Mexican Jesuit and historian Francisco Javier Clavijero and the Prussian geographer Alexander von Humboldt, among others. Incidentally, it was a letter written by a Jesuit missionary, reporting the presence of a rare independent visitor whom they suspected to be a Papal spy at the imperial court in Beijing, that ultimately silenced allegations of inauthenticity (Doria, 2000). But one must bear in mind that authorship was differently conceived at that time, which would have made accusations of academic plagiarism anachronistic. Gemelli Careri's methodology involved intertextual practices, using the writings of previous and/or contemporary men of letters to augment his observations (Loureiro, 2014). He also fashioned himself as a learned traveller, intellectually equipped for the voyage: "*non farà fuor di proposito aver letto tutte le Relazioni, che si sono pubblicate de paesi, che si voglion camminare, como altresí le loro Istorie*"[6] (in Loureiro, 2014: 12). Not unlike Pigafetta and Carletti, whose pursuit of knowledge was accompanied by the desire to disseminate it, Gemelli Careri took the process a step further and adopted a didactic habitus. As mentioned in the previous chapter, this pedagogic slant likely arises from his recognition of travel literature's potential as an instrument not just of learning but also of teaching (Buccini, 1996: 255), that is, "travel as a pedagogic tool" (Monga, 1996: 19).

Carletti's and Gemelli Careri's accounts would suffer a different fate in Filipino scholarship, as opposed to their general success in Europe, but also, and perhaps more notably, in contrast with Pigafetta's ubiquity in Philippine historiography. For instance, the only available material relating to Gemelli Careri in the library of the country's national university, the University of the Philippines, is a 1963 publication of the *Giro*'s 1744 English translation. Only the part relating to the Philippine Islands (Vol. 5) was included in this publication. In his introduction to this volume, Garcia (1963) makes a note of Gemelli Careri's absence in Philippine historiography:

> To many local readers, Careri is an unknown entity, and it is doubted if even local scholars can pretend to know his book. This is not surprising, however, if we note that even well-known Philippine bibliographers fare no better, as witness the fact that even Retana and Pardo de Tavera appear not to have been acquainted with it.
>
> (p. xv)

Carletti's *Ragionamenti*, on the other hand, is yet to be published as an edition or a new translation by a Filipino publisher. Why the Filipiniana Book Guild chose to reprint the *Giro* and not the *Ragionamenti* is unclear, considering Carletti's virtual invisibility among local scholars. We may conjecture that this is owing to the considerably shorter length of Carletti's account. This bibliographic lacuna would be filled by the Philippine–Italian Association, which published a 26-page reprint of the Manila leg of Francesco Carletti's journey (Part Six of the First Discourse on the West Indies) "*che tratta del viaggio fatto dal Messico all'isole Filippine per via d'Acapulco, e del successo in quella navicatione*"[7] (Carletti, 1958: XIX). This edition was translated by the Italian diplomat and orientalist Giuliano Bertuccioli and published by the Philippine-Italian Association in 1979 bearing the title "A Florentine in Manila." It is important to note that this nonprofit, cross-cultural organisation is the same one that commissioned a Filipino national artist to build a Pigafetta statue in the 1970s, highlighting the integral role that Italian travel literature plays in bridging cultural ties between Italy and the Philippines.

On the same European trip during which Rizal unearthed Pigafetta's manuscript among the countless archives that he had within reach, the impassioned *ilustrado* also got acquainted with other European observers who had ventured to the Philippine Islands, including Gemelli Careri. In Mojares' (2002) historiographical study, the author of the *Giro* is mentioned only once, relegated to a list of names that were of interest to the national hero:

> [Rizal] immersed himself in sources relating to the Philippines – the Spanish missionary reports of Gaspar de San Agustin, Pedro Chirino, Francisco Colin, and Diego Aduarte, and such historical and travel books as those of Jagor, Bartolome de Argensola, Alfred Marche, and Gemelli Careri.
>
> (Mojares, 2002: 55)

We may liken José Rizal to his Italian namesake and fellow itinerant scholar Joseph Barletti, who endeavoured to demystify and contest exogenous writings that conjured inaccurate portraits of his homeland and those who people it. Whereas Pigafetta's *Relazione* has been subject to much literary and historiographical investigation in the Philippine academe, the *Giro* has exclusively been studied as a historical source, as in Manzano's (2013) study of the Manila

Galleon's value in colonial Philippine society. In Mojares' (2013: 58) reconstruction of lay knowledge about the Philippines, Gemelli Careri is cited only once, owing to the Calabrian's fantastical description of a tailed native. Worse still, Carletti's name is absent from Rizal's archival inventory and remains an obscure primary source in Philippine scholarship, understudied by historians and literary scholars alike. The notable imbalance of local interest directed towards the three travel accounts may be explained not so much by their textual properties, such as the narrative style or rhetorical strategies employed by their authors, but by their respective place in the timeline of Philippine history. The Pigafetta chronicle (1521) is positioned at the confluence of ancient "Philippine" civilisation and the Spanish civilising mission. Carletti's sojourn in Manila (1596) occurred two decades after the formal establishment of a colonial settlement in 1571, exactly 50 years post-"discovery." Gemelli Careri's testimony, written a century after Carletti's voyage, was already situated within an intricate colonial society. The visibly greater emphasis placed upon the *Relazione* by Filipino academics is thus a result of the text's weight in Philippine history. Whereas the *Ragionamenti and Giro* are mere parts of a hefty inventory of Western sources about Philippine colonisation, the *Relazione* is the "preeminent text of discovery" that featured the Islands on the cusp of colonisation (Mojares, 2002: 20).

Studying travel literature about the archipelago, contemporary Filipino scholars take cue from the Filipino cosmopolitan intellectuals who, in the late nineteenth century, weaved from periphery to centre and read Western epistemology as a counterpoint to indigenous ontology. The *ilustrados*' scholarly activities in pursuit of national consciousness signify "instances of colonized subjects defracting power" (Rabasa, 1993: 11–12). The next chapter will tease out the similarities and differences in the three "Italian" chroniclers' semiotic creation of the "Filipino" colonised subjects, while carefully accounting for the spatial and temporal divergences between their travels and the ambivalent subjectivity of "Italian" travellers as liminal figures themselves, whose pursuit of knowledge and textual production were valuable to the Empire, but whose lack of a national origin cast them as the Empire's internal Others. A twofold examination of Italian travel writing in the Philippines will be put forward in the next chapter. As a counterpoint to the postcolonial reading of their epistemic violence towards the "Filipino" subject, the "Italian" travellers' liminality as manifest (or elided) in their texts will also be interrogated.

Notes

1 "First trip around the world / by the Chevalier Pigafetta; aboard the squadron of Magellan, during the years 1519, 20, 21, and 22; followed by an excerpt on Chevalier Martin Behaim; with the description of his globe; with maps and figures."

2 See Cachey, Jr. (2007), and Vanon (2019) for an exhaustive and updated bibliographic history of the *Relazione*.

3 Have one of those there learn Italian because I have Italian manuscripts here that deal with the first arrival of the Spaniards to the Philippines: they were written by a companion of Magellan, and since I don't have time to translate them on account of my many tasks, it would be good if a fellow countryman could translate them into Tagalog or Spanish so that it can be known how we were in 1520. Italian is easy, one can learn it in a month with the Ahn Method. Now I am learning Dutch.

4 "Reflections of the Florentine F.C. on things that he had seen in his travels, in the West and East Indies, as in other Countries."

5 See Dei (1987) for a complete list of the Italian editions and Sgrilli (1906) for a comprehensive bibliographic study.

6 "[I]t would not be inopportune to have read all the Relations that had been published about the country that one wishes to visit, as well as its Histories."

7 "About the voyage from Mexico to the Philippine Islands by way of Acapulco and that which took place in that navigation."

Reference list

Blair, E. H., & Robertson, J. A. (1902). Preface. In E. H. Blair & J. A. Robertson (Eds.), *The Philippine Islands, 1493–1898* (Vol. I, pp. 89–96). Arthur H. Clark Company.

Brege, B. (2021). *Tuscany in the age of empire*. Harvard University Press.

Bourne, G. E. (1902). Historical introduction. In E. H. Blair & J.A. Robertson (Eds.), *The Philippine Islands, 1493–1898* (Vol. I, pp. 19–88). Arthur H. Clark Company.

Buccini, S. (1996). Coerenza metodologica nel "Giro del mondo" di Giovanni Francesco Gemelli Careri. *Annali d'Italianistica*, *14*, 246–256.

Cachey Jr., T. J. (Ed.). (2007). Bio-bibliographical note. In T. J. Cachey, L. Ballerini & M. Ciavolella (Eds.), *First voyage around the world (1519–1522): An account of Magellan's expedition* (pp. xxxvii–lvi). University of Toronto Press.

Cano, G. (2008). Blair and Robertson's "The Philippine Islands, 1493–1898": Scholarship or imperialist propaganda? *Philippine Studies*, *56*(1), 3–46.

Carletti, F. (1958). *Ragionamenti del mio viaggio al mondo*. Giulio Einaudi editore.

Colla, E. (2008). 16th Century Japan and Macau described by Francesco Carletti (1573?–1636). *Bulletin of Portuguese-Japanese Studies*, *17*, 113–144.

Dei, A. (1987). Nota bio-bibliografica. In F. Carletti (Ed.), *Ragionamenti del mio viaggio intorno al mondo* (pp. 21–23). Ugo Mursia Editore.

Doria, P. (2000). Gemelli Careri, Giovanni Franesco. In *Enciclopedia Treccani: Dizionario Biografico degli Italiani* (Vol. 53). www.treccani.it/enciclopedia/gemelli-careri-giovanni-francesco_(Dizionario-Biografico)

Garcia, M. (1963). G. F. Gemelli Careri. In *A Voyage to the Philippines* (Vol. 2). Filipiniana Book Guild.

Guha, P., & Diaz, L. (2020). A Forest of National Histories: An Interview with Lav Diaz. *Cinéaste*, *45*(3), 20–25. https://www.jstor.org/stable/26976390

Guillermo, R. (2017). Andres Bonifacio: proletarian hero of the Philippines and Indonesia. *Inter-Asia Cultural Studies*, *18*(3), 338–346. https://doi.org/10.1080/14649373.2017.1350498

Loureiro, R. (2014). Traveling experiences vs. intertextuality. *Anais de História de Além-Mar*, *15*, 101–136.

Manzano, D. (2013). Gemelli and his travel to the Philippines. *Asian Perspectives in the Arts and Humanities*, *3*(1), 101–122.

Maaruf, S. (2022). *Concept of a hero in Malay society*. Strategic Information and Research Development Centre.

McCarl, C. (2019). The transmission and bibliographic study of the Pigafetta account: Synthesis and update. *Abriu: Estudos de textualidade do Brasil, Galicia e Portugal*, *8*, 85–98.

Mojares, R. B. (2002). *Waiting for mariang makiling: Essays in philippine cultural history*. Ateneo University Press.

Mojares, R. B. (2006). Brains of the nation: Pedro Paterno. *TH Pardo de Javera, Isabelo de los Reyes and the Production of Modern Knowledge*, Quezon City: Ateneo de Manila.

Mojares, R. B. (2013). *Isabelo's archive*. Anvil Publishing, Inc.

Monga, L. (1996). Travel and Travel Writing: An Historical Overview of Hodoeporics. *Annali d'italianistica*, *14*, 6–54.

Morga, A. (1609). *Sucesos de las Islas Filipinas*. Casa de Geronymo Balli.

Nery, J. (2011). *Revolutionary spirit: Jose Rizal in Southeast Asia*. Institute of Southeast Asian Studies.

Rabasa, J. (1993). *Inventing America: Spanish historiography and the formation of Eurocentrism* (Vol. 11). University of Oklahoma Press.

Rizal, J. (1889, February 4). [Letter to M. H. Del Pilar]. Correspondencia Epistolar. Cartas entre Rizal y sus colegas de la Propaganda (1961). *Comisión Nacional del Centenerio de José Rizal (Escritos de José Rizal, Tomo II, Libro Tercero, Primera Parte)*. https://www.cervantesvirtual.com/obra/cartas-entre-rizal-y-sus-colegas-de-la-propaganda/

Sgrilli, G. (1906). *Francesco Carletti, mercante e viaggiatore fiorentino* (Vol. 6). L. Cappelli.

Sloterdijk, P. (2013). *In the world interior of capital: Towards a philosophical theory of globalization*. Polity.

Szönyi, G. E. (2018). Broadening horizons of renaissance humanism from the antiquity to the new world. *Primerjalna književnost*, *41*(2).

Vagnon, E. (2010). De la Grèce antique au voyage de Magellan. Les modèles humanistes d'Antonio Pigafetta et de Maximilianus Transylvanus. Médiévales. *Langues, Textes, Histoire*, *58*, 99–111.

5 The "Filipino" native according to the "Italian" chronicler

Ethnography is an indispensable facet of the literature of travel, just as contact with alterity is an inescapable element of travel itself. After all, the observer in transit cannot but set foot on domains that have been peopled long before the newcomer's arrival. Combing through travelogues deposited in the colonial archive reveals the voyagers' ethnographic impulse as they meticulously sketched, in writing, the territories visited. They listed the flora and fauna present, described the inhabitants encountered, took stock of the natives' relationship with local biota, their customs, languages, and forms of social organisation (Rubiés, 2002: 1). In this chapter, we shall interrogate how the Venetian Pigafetta, the Tuscan Carletti, and the Calabrian Gemelli Careri pursued this ethnographic impulse through their representation of the peoples that inhabited the Philippine Islands at different but not so disparate junctures. Even as their chronicles were inscribed within the vast repertoire of early modern European travel writing, each account was produced under distinct configurations along the Philippine historical timeline on one hand, and the Italian historical timeline on the other. To emphasise the heterogeneity of colonial-era travel literature, this examination of the "Italian" travellers' interpretation of difference as it transpires in their rhetorical construction of the "Filipino" native does not discount the former's ambivalent subjectivity. Put simply, while the semiotic creation of the colonised subject (Rabasa, 1993) occupies a prominent place in the following analysis, the itinerant subject's unique positionality merits equal attention. After all, this monograph's unique engagement with analogous scholarship on Italian travel is the bringing of Hester's (2003, 2016) and Cachey's (1996) observed "placelessness" of Italian literary identity into the realm of postcolonial critique, while nuancing Philippine historiography's oftentimes monolithic treatment of colonial-era travel writing by the West. As we examine how the three Italian chroniclers used the familiar to interpret the alterity of the "Filipino" indigenes, it is important to steer clear of the "crucial contradiction that Orientalism embodies" (Porter, 2015: 153), namely, the essentialising of colonial discourse. By asking what constitutes the familiar and where it derives from, we can unpack how the travel writer's

DOI: 10.4324/9781032722320-6

persona, the "I narrator," evolves into an implicit "we" as he engages in the discursive construction of "they."

5.1 The "I" narrator

From the Middle Ages to its early modern European elaborations, the textualisation of travel was marked by certain characteristics, most notably the salience of the "*io narrante*" 'I, narrator' (Nelli, 2009: 2). In his opening dedication to his benefactor, Pigafetta adopted a rhetorical strategy that would come to dictate his narration. "The first-person authorial perspective" (Mojares, 2002: 24) established the chronicler's authority as a rightful observer as if by divine ordinance:

> *Perchè sono molti curiosi, illustrissimo ed eccellentissimo signor, che non solamente se contentano de sapere e intendere le grandi ed ammirabili cose che Dio me ha concesso di vedere e patire ne la infrascritta mia longa e pericolosa navigazione, ma ancora vogliono sapere li mezzi e modi e vie che ho tenuto ad andarvi, non prestando quella integra fede a l'esito se prima non hanno bona certezza de l'inizio.*[1]
>
> (Pigafetta, 1956: 8)

His observations are imbued with literary flair in the "epic-heroic style" of "chivalric romance" (Field, 2006: 328). From a formalistic standpoint, Pigafetta's authorial voice resonates that of a Castiglione courtier who embodied "*discretione*" 'dignity and restraint' as he looked upon his surroundings with a gaze that was neither "dominating [nor] acquisitive" (Mojares, 2002: 41). Yet despite professing personal curiosity and desire for posterity as his main motives for embarking on the Magellan expedition, Pigafetta repeatedly demonstrates reverence to the captain. This cements his chronicle to the Portuguese explorer's legendary quest:

> *Tutti allegri lo supplicorono volesse lasciarli due uomini, o almeno uno, acciò li ammaestrasse ne la fede e che li farebbero grande onore. Gli rispose che allora non poteva lasciarli alcuno, ma se volevano essere Cristiani, lo prete nostro li battezzerebbe, e che un'altra fiata menaria preti e frati, che li insegnerebbero la fede nostra. Risposero che prima volevano parlare al re e poi diventarebbero Cristiani. Lagrimassemo tutti per la grande allegrezza.*[2]
>
> (Pigafetta, 1956: 79–80)

Indeed, the *Relazione* has a deeper evangelical imprint than Carletti's *Ragionamenti* or Gemelli Careri's *Giro*. Several times, the narrator expresses sentiments intimately linked with the expedition's overt aim to convert the "heathen" indigenes. As such, while his gaze is not overtly colonising thanks to the subtlety of his narration and his humanist-oriented language, there are slippages in his narrative that betray a missionary posture. There is greater similarity between Pigafetta's "I, narrator" and that of Gemelli Careri's, notwithstanding the two centuries that separate their travels. The same authorial perspective is observable in the *Giro*. The Calabrian globetrotter situates himself in an authoritative position as he begins to cite his observations about the Islands and his musings on the inhabitants. Just as Pigafetta framed his testimony as the product of a long and perilous journey, so did Gemelli Careri profess his nonpassive love for knowledge by readily embarking on a hazardous quest.

> *[E]d avendo ormai, colla sperienza, apparato à soffrire i patimenti, che ne' lunghi viaggi si incontrano; deliberai, senz'altro indugio interporre, passar da Macao all'Isole Filippine . . . per espormi quindi alla più pericolosa navigazione, che immaginar si possa; e che per lo spazio di sette mesi, fecemi bersaglio di fiere, a spaventevoli tempeste.*[3]
>
> (Gemelli Careri, 1700: 2)

Both travellers stressed their steadfast curiosity against all odds, embodying the modern navigator's "habitus" in their conviction that they had been mandated to recount their experiences in the wider world upon their homecoming (Sloterdijk, 2013: 38). Contrary to the courtier's studied nonchalance which Pigafetta's "I, narrator" personified, Gemelli Careri opens his voyage to the Philippine archipelago with a verbose admonition of sloth:

> *Egli si è tanta, e sì grande la dignità, ed eccellenza dell'umana natura, e cotanto attiva la virtù delle scintille di quel celeste fuoco di cui partecipa; che molto dappoco, ed indegni d'essere appellati uomini, devono riputarsi coloro, i quali, o per pusillanimità, da essi chiamata prudenza; o per pigrizia, che dicono moderazione; o in fine, per avarizia, cui dan nome d'iconomica, dalle gloriose, e chiare azioni, per qualunque modo s'arretrano. Molti senza dubbio, le difficili imprese, da altrui generosamente recate à fine, volentieri, con istudiate parole, e in rima, e in prosa, fino alle stelle s'ingegnano d'innalzare; ma pochissimi poi, per giugnere a cotal laude, le loro operazioni indrizzar vogliono.*[4]
>
> (Gemelli Careri, 1700: 7)

This introduction reads as a self-exaltation thinly disguised as a reprimand. One may interpret his self-professed virtue as "idle pride," which Monga (1996: 35) lists as a likely ramification of contact with the Other which often triggers a crisis in the Self's value system. Alternatively or in addition to that, Buccini (1996) reads it as the author's recognition of travel writing's didactic value. Although the *Giro* is not strictly a treatise, its pedagogical ethos and methodological coherence place it within the narrative tradition of eighteenth-century travel (Guglielminetti, 2015: 55). The evolution of travel literature from the Middle Ages to its early modern iterations brought novel writing strategies and ulterior purposes (Nelli, 2009). Absent from Pigafetta's mode of narration is Gemelli Careri's fusion of prior knowledge with his personal observations, and the vision to offer guidance to future voyagers.

Deviating from the authorial supremacy performed by Pigafetta and Gemelli Careri, Carletti openly admits to relying on sheer memory as he staged his experiences in the fixity of print. The *Ragionamenti*'s narratorial premises were grounded on its author's conversations with his patron. This accounts for the chronicle's dialogic style as the Grand Duke specifically mandated Carletti to put his oral testimonies into writing. Since his memoranda had been confiscated by Dutch authorities along with his merchandise, Carletti wrote his account retrospectively. This is a significant distinction from the synchronicity of the voyage and its documentation, which differentiates the *Ragionamenti* from the *Relazione* and the *Giro*. Thus, Carletti's performance as traveller/observer is staged in two different planes, first orally and then in print, unveiling the mediated process of documenting travel (Motsch, 2011: 215). Not only its mode of "telling" but also its narrative style reads distinctive. Unlike Pigafetta, who was influenced by courtly romance (Mojares, 2002) and explored the marvellous trope (Testa-de Ocampo, 2010), or Gemelli Careri with his Petrarcan leitmotifs (Hester, 2011, 2016) and didactic approach (Buccini, 1996), Careri's narration is precise to the point of terseness. His primary occupation was that of a merchant. The pragmaticism of his discourse is visible in his fixed gaze on elements of indigenous spaces that could spark commercial interest. The sparse literariness of his text transposes it in the repertoire of seventeenth-century scientific prose (Silvestro, 1958: XII), which primed objectivity over rhetoric in contrast with the dominant poetics that shaped Pigafetta and Gemelli Careri as travel writers, each distinct from one another. Yet to reduce the *Ragionamenti* to a practical trader's report is not only to ignore its value in that epoch's scholarly enterprise, but also to cast it outside the sphere of literary writing (Perocco, 1997: 22). In this vein, we can inscribe Carletti's text within the literary strand of merchant writers who wilfully and self-consciously participated in knowledge production through the privileged position of mobility accorded to them by their profession.

As self-financed globetrotters, Carletti and Gemelli Careri cannot be described as participant observers (to use contemporary ethnographic categories). Their accounts therefore cast a distancing layer between the "I, narrator" and the narrative's course of action that would have been impossible in the case of Pigafetta, whose discursive allegiance to the *capitano generale* lent his chronicle a sense of belonging to the imperial mission. However, it must be noted that Gemelli Careri's diaristic modality has greater similarity with Pigafetta's authorial perspective than with Carletti's dialogic model. Even as the Florentine merchant converses with the Grand Duke, we rarely witness his active participation in the scenarios that unfold. Thus, the seeming "objectivity" of his observations comes as a result of the rhetorical strategy of agent deletion and self-effacement (Pratt, 1985: 183). The different personal and political contexts that shaped their travel, alongside the varied literary contexts that influenced their writing, result in a multitone of narratorial voices, justifying why "Italian" travel writing about the colonial Philippines must not be treated as a monolithic textual production. Let us now shift the plane of discourse to the "Italian" chroniclers' interpretation of difference, taking cues from Philippine scholarship on travel literature which has probed the Western discursive invention of the "Filipino."

5.2 The discursive "they"

One colonialist mode of representation is the apparently unassuming way of collectively naming their subjects of observation (Spurr, 1993: 4). In his *Relazione*, Pigafetta uses "those people"[5] to refer to the islanders. With this appellation, the islanders are homogenised, stripped of their individuality, and reduced to a collective "they." By doing so, Pigafetta carries out the ulterior ends of the "rhetoric of othering" (Jasinski, 2001: 412), of which travel literature is an eminent example. That is, by creating a semiotic "they," European narrators contemporaneously build identity and assimilate the aboriginal inhabitants into a single mass that can easily be moulded into an object of knowledge (Pratt, 1985: 143). However, several times throughout the Philippine leg of the Magellan–Elcano expedition, the narrator of the *Relazione* appears to deviate from dichotomous othering. Pigafetta uses similes to suggest a faint similarity between the indigenous culture and his own. Mojares (2002) calls it a "double movement," which served to inform Magellan's colonising motive: "Likeness suggests that these are a people with whom Europeans can have intercourse; difference demands that they be subjected to the levelling, 'civilizing' power of Europe" (p. 33).

> *Il re ne volse tener seco a cena; li dicessemo non potevamo allora restare. Pigliata la licenza, il principe ne menò seco a casa sua, dove sonavano quattro fanciulle, una de tamburo a modo nostro, ma era posta in terra; un'altra dava con un legno, fatto alquanto grosso nel capo con tela de palma, in due borchie piccate, uno in l'uno, uno in l'altro: l'altra in una borchia grande col medesimo modo.*[6]
>
> (Pigafetta, 1956: 83–84)

The suggestion of likeness which, at first glance, appears to double-cross the rhetoric of empire, is likely the result of his quasi-ethnographic immersion in indigenous life. Pigafetta's invitation to a gathering at a chieftain's abode accorded his observations a level of intimacy that is unparalleled in other places visited, and which neither Carletti nor Gemelli Careri, as autonomous travellers, would be privy to.

The "exotic" body is another site of the investigation of alterity and its interpretation through the lens of the familiar. The *Relazione* reveals its narrator's desire to unveil that which is usually hidden from his cultural provenance.

> *Queste erano assai belle e bianche, quasi come le nostre e così grandi . . . erano nude, se non che avevano tela de arbore da la cinta fino al ginocchio, e alcune tutte nude, col picchietto de le orecchie grande, con un cerchietto de legno dentro, che lo tiene tondo e largo; con li capelli grandi e negri, e con uno velo piccolo attorno al capo, e sempre discalze.*[7]
>
> (Pigafetta, 1956: 83–84)

The quasi similarity that Pigafetta observes between the female islanders and their European counterparts imposes on the former a framework of beauty that will never apply to them by virtue of racial difference, as evidenced in the levelling of beauty and whiteness which is betrayed in his text. In his elaborate description of a sexual act, Pigafetta accords his Western audience visual access to the "Filipino" native's body, hence opening it up to the gaze, a modality of sighting underpinned by an element of desire and predicated on an asymmetrical relationship that concedes power to the beholder of the gaze. Indeed, the "disempowering" gaze of the male spectator and that of the imperial observer "are overlapping and intersecting when sight is directed at the other" (Jones, 2011: 110).

> *Questi popoli vanno nudi; portano solamente uno pezzo de tela de palme attorno le sue vergogne. Grandi e piccoli hanno passato il suo membro, circa de la testa, da l'una parte all'altra con uno ferro de oro, ovvero de stagno, grosso come una penna de oca. . . . Assaissime volte lo volsi vedere da molti, così vecchi come giovani, perchè non lo poteva credere. . . . Loro dicono che le sue moglie voleno così, e, se fossero d'altra sorte, non usariano con elli. Quando questi voleno usare con le femmine, loro medesime lo pigliano non in ordine, e cominciano pian piano a mettersi dentro prima quella stella de sovra e poi l'altra. Quando è dentro, diventa in ordine, e così sempre sta dentro fin che diventa molle, perchè altramente non lo porriano cavare fuora. Questi popoli usano questo, perchè sono de debile natura.*[8]
>
> (Pigafetta, 1956: 99)

For such a scrupulous observer, neither does the male body escape from Pigafetta's gaze. Here, it is not beauty that is weighed against Western aesthetic ideals, but masculine virility. Faced with such "strange and diabolic ways" (as Carletti would later describe while witnessing the same act), Pigafetta imposes a judgment to conclude his "exotic" testimony with a semblance of logical reasoning. He resorts to essentialising the native male subjects, reasoning that "these peoples" are weak by nature and using it as preface to the following remark that unbosoms "colonial desire":

> *Hanno quante moglie voleno, ma una principale. Se uno dei nostri andava in terra, così come de dì come de notte, ognuno lo convitava perchè mangiasse e bevesse. Le sue vivande sono mezze cotte e molto salate; bevono spesso e molto con quelli sui cannuti da li vasi; e dura cinque o sei ore uno suo mangiare. Le donne amavano assai più noi che questi. A tutte, da sei anni in su, li aprono la natura a poco a poco per cagion de quelli suoi membri.*[9]
>
> (Pigafetta, 1956: 53)

As a humanist scholar aboard an expansionist expedition, Pigafetta's curiosity was entrenched in "colonial desire," that is, the notion that sexuality cannot be divorced from the imperial paradigm (Young, 1995). Colonialism and its operative discourses as pregnant with desire occurs in two planes, both in the colonial iconography of virgin (hence, female) territories ripe for (European male) conquest (Mieu, 2015) and in the constitution of the "sexed subaltern subject" (Spivak, 1988). Although he is not the first "Italian" traveller to foray into representations of the sexual uncanny, Pigafetta's "preeminent text of discovery" (Mojares, 2002: 20) unveiled the archipelago to the European imaginary and served as the literary pretext to its conquest. This clearly cements his travelogue within the civilising mission. As already mentioned, Pigafetta's ethnography of the "Filipino" native is rife with ambivalence and, in this particular instance, the evangelising posture that he adopts every time a "heathen" is converted to Christianity strikes a discordant note with his discursive performance of a Western male who automatically assumes a superior status as a result of the ontological weakness, physically and morally, of the male "Other".

Interestingly, Carletti's take on the same native custom reveals a less desirous but more moralistic slant, which confirms Hester's (2016) observation that the Florentine merchant, although travelling independently and generally assuming a disenchanted gaze, was still informed by a Eurocentric worldview. Arriving at an already established colony, Carletti does not acquire the power of the gaze by virtue of being a welcomed guest. Abiding by the *ragion di mercatura*, he pays for the "exotic" sight in the same way a tourist nowadays would purchase a ticket to witness an indigenous spectacle. This is in sharp contrast with Pigafetta's active agential voice, as he spoke of directly asking the male natives to show him their pierced members.

> *Li popoli bisaios sono uomini tutti deditissimi alli piaceri di Venere, e le loro donne non sono meno innamorate che belle, con le quali si trastullano in diverse e strane e diaboliche maniere; e spetialmente una, che se io non l'avessi vista non ardirei raccontarla a V. A. S. per non esser tenuto mendace, ma poiché io, per curiosità e per certificarmene, spesi anche qualche danari accioché mi fosse mostrato quello che m'era stato detto, mi si può dunque prestar fede. Questi bisaios o la piu parte di loro, per inventione del diavolo e per dare e avere diabolico piacere con le loro donne, usano forarsi il membro virile. . . . Questo modo di lussuriare dicono essere*

> *stato ritrovato da loro per sanità, ciò è per aver manco occasione di usare Venere e tener piu satie le loro femine; ma so dire anco per aggiunta che piu tosto sia una pura inventione di satanasso, per impedire la generatione umana a questi sgratiati.*[10]
>
> (Carletti, 1958: 92–93)

In his testimony, he appears to flaunt to the Grand Duke the balance between his spirit of inquiry and his moral compass. Beholding the radically unfamiliar leads him to the rhetorical strategy of essentialising the native, as Pigafetta did, albeit Carletti does so by inserting Christian-oriented judgments and reducing the native tradition of genital piercing to the Devil's work. Still, the distanced tone remains through his syntactic strategy of employing passive verbs (rather than "I think" or "I believe"), while his subjective discernment is couched in adjectival phrases that characterise "those wretched people." Hearsay also figures as a key element in his observations, and his frequent utterance of "they say" or "I had been told" serves his self-effacing tactic. In the *Ragionamenti*, Carletti uses several collective appellations, interchanging between "*(quei) popoli*" 'those peoples,' "*(quell')indiani*" 'those Indians,' and the occasional "*barbari*" 'barbarians,' which he exclusively uses when describing misfortunes involving natives.

A further discursive technique in representing Otherness is to minimise the difference among the subaltern, since the conquerable or conquered natives are represented as generic beings stripped of individual subjectivity (JanMohamed, 1985: 85). All three chroniclers displayed at once homogenising and essentialising tendencies in their rhetoric. In the *Relazione*, Pigafetta (1956) paints a picture of a peace-loving people, predisposed to tranquillity and leisure ("*amano la pace, l'ozio e la quiete*" [p. 85]). Even with a seemingly positive description, the natives remain subject to the rhetoric of othering – once again because these subjects are abstracted and are suspended in an "infinite present tense" (Pratt, 1985: 139), which isolates their actions from any circumstantial or historical context. The way they behave must necessarily be dictated by their innate qualities. In the *Relazione*, the islanders are characterised as lovers of peace and tranquillity to the point of idleness. Pigafetta does not retract or contradict this statement when he recounts the battle of Mactan that led to his much-admired captain's untimely death; instead, "those people" retain their pacific disposition. This renders them alluring objects of conquest, as it hints at the possibility of their passive "consent," which was highly coveted during the dominant phase of colonialism where the conquered were yanked into the conqueror's sphere of influence through military and bureaucratic subjugation (JanMohamed, 1985: 61).

The Philippine part of the *Ragionamenti* is curiously devoid of credit to Pigafetta's *Relazione*, despite the latter being the founding Western testimony of the archipelago. This does not foreclose references in Carletti's chronicle to Pigafetta's textual production over half a century earlier. For instance,

Carletti refers to the Marianas Islands by stating that the Spanish call it "[*isla*] *de las Velas o vero Ladrones*" (1958: 79), which Pigafetta had denominated thusly on one of the rudimentary maps that appeared in his chronicle. We might recall that colonial maps did not only charter spaces ripe for conquering; they also embedded exogenous labels onto native domains, heralding new landscapes of power while textualising places according to the European imaginary (Ashcroft et al., 2013). Pigafetta superimposed foreign notions of transaction and property when he referred to the first European geographical reference of the Pacific as "*l'Isola dei ladroni*" 'the Island of Thieves.' By inscribing these novel names in writing, colonial geographers and explorers effectively transformed already inhabited places into terra nullius, performing an act of erasure through superimposition. Carletti (1958) even confirms the accuracy of the place names, which again essentialises the Othered subjects, confirming cartography's semiotic potential (pp. 71–72):

> *[Isola] de los Latrones. Nomi appropriatoli, il primo per la grandissima quantità delle barchette, che si veddero uscire da esse isole per quel mare, tutte a vela, su bito che quell'isolani ebbero veduta la nostra nave, che parea coprissero il mare d'ogni intorno.*

Although a voluminous part of the *Ragionamenti* is dedicated to an inventory of the biota and commerce of his destinations, the merchant's ethnographic impulse remains present. He echoes his predecessor's essentialising observation of a gentle people driven by worldly pleasures, such as gambling ("*si passano il tempo, con far combattere i galli*"[11] [Carletti, 1958: 92]) and sex ("*Li popoli bisaios sono uomini tutti deditissimi alli piaceri di Venere*"[12] [Carletti, 1958: 92]). Another rhetorical parallelism between Pigafetta and Carletti is their displayed reticence in affirming native skill. We might recall the former's restraint in praising the natives' musical ability, as if in doing so he would be attributing artistic faculty to "these people": "*facevano un soave suono. Tanto a tempo sonavano, che pareva avessero gran ragion del canto*"[13] (Pigafetta, 1956: 83). Instead, Pigafetta recognises a potential or an inclination through the neutral, passive verb "*parere*" 'to appear/seem.' Navigating in the archipelago, Carletti witnessed the islanders' aquatic dexterity:

> *[Q]uelli Indiani che andavano nuotando per il mare, non si lassando vedere per la paura che avevano delle archibusiate, s'ascondevano sotto la nostra nave, talora uscendo fuor del l'acqua da una banda, talora dall'altra, per repigliare il fiato, e subito si rituffavano, essendo in questo tanto eccellenti nuotatori che non hanno invidia a'pesci. . . . Cosa certo di maravigliosa destrezza e stupore, ma che maraviglia, se questi uomini sempre stanno in sul mare e vivono del pescare in quello? O sia come molti dicono, che lo faccino per fatturie o incantesimi?*[14]
>
> (Carletti, 1958: 84)

The attitude he adopts appears more dismissive than Pigafetta's, since he outright challenges why native skill should be striking when it may be explained as a function of their geographical setting. In this instance, however, the essentialist rhetoric proves insufficient as a discursive strategy to downplay the Other's faculties. By raising the second rhetorical question, Carletti shifts the plane of interpretation to the dimension of the supernatural, thus questioning the logical coherence of a masterful Other. We will see this essentialising tactic more acutely in Gemelli Careri's *Giro*, whose Philippine account is much heftier than Pigafetta's or Carletti's.

Studying the contents of the *Giro*'s fifth volume raises the question as to how the chronicler covered a wide breadth of Philippine life with as much attention to detail in his six-week stay at the colonial capital. This time was not even dedicated to extensive travel, as Gemelli Careri dealt with tedious embarking and disembarking procedures when he was not mingling with political and religious personalities of Manila's "*alta sociedad*" 'high society' (Loureiro, 2014: 113). The *Giro*'s narrator collectively refers to the inhabitants as "indians." A look at the six-volume account reveals that the author does not uniformly employ this terminology. In fact, the term "indian" is only deployed in the last two volumes, i.e., Volumes V and VI concerning the Philippine Islands and New Spain. Here, Gemelli Careri situates himself in the epistemological zeitgeist in which Western, specifically Spanish, observers ascribe inferior intellectual and cultural development to Amerindian and Philippine "indios" (De Acosta & Mateos, 1999). Indeed, he placed emphasis on the empire rather than the inhabitants in his other travel destinations, writing of "the territorial boundaries of the Ottoman Empire," "the trade riches of the Great Mogul," or "the characters of the Chinese, their genius and ability in the liberal arts, and their fundamental books." The eulogising tone with which he writes of the peoples of the longstanding empires he visited reads as a stark contrast to the barbarising undercurrents that flow beneath his writings of colonised spaces. This duality is especially manifest in the index of the *Giro*'s last volume with no mention of the ancient Mesoamerican civilisation but with a chapter on the "horrible sacrifices that the Indians do for their idols." The concurrence of a negative qualifier with the collective label "indians" unmasks the positionality of the voyager–narrator. To refer to the natives of the Philippine Islands and those of New Spain as "indians" is to depict them as peoples still in the process of becoming "civilised."

His essentialist rhetoric is most salient in the chapter on "the language, character, and customs of the indians of the Philippine Islands" where he provides copious details of indigenous life. Still, his elaborate ethnology boils down to an affermation of the "Filipino" native's idleness.

> *La sola pigrizia non fa comparire il lor buon talento; ed ha preso così altamente a dominargli, che se, incamminando, sentissero pungersi i'piedi da qualche spina; per non prendere la fatica di calarsi, non la torrebbono da quel luogo, acciò gl'altri non v'inciampassero.*[15]
>
> (Gemelli Careri, 1700: 14)

Gemelli Careri (1700) does not merely allude to this predisposition as Pigafetta and Carletti did, but highlights it: "*Dopo il dominio Spagnuolo si sono fatti tutti pigri, quantunque riescano ne' lavori meccanici; come in far cateniglie, e Rosari d'oro dilicatissimi, ed altre cose*"[16] (p. 140). While his descriptions are framed in the "infinite present tense," his temporal designation hints at a possible causality between Spanish colonisation and the infamous Filipino indolence.[17] Despite their rhetorical essentialism and homogenisation, all three chroniclers portrayed certain contrasts among the native population, although their observed distinctions arise from various factors. Documenting native heterogeneity does not necessarily constitute a departure from the rhetoric of othering. Nuances permeate all types of discourse and the fluctuating shades of representation that are present in some, if not most, travelogues should not be simplistically read as mere deviations from colonialist writing. After all, colonial discourse must not be understood as a monolithic, static, and continuously coherent structure of representation, since it reflects the fissures and slippages that permeate the very establishment it serves (Spurr, 1993: 11). In the *Relazione*, the observable distinction among natives is rooted in social ranking.

> *Nella isola de questo re, che condussi a le navi, se trova pezzi de oro, grandi come noci e uovi, crivellando la terra. Tutti li vasi de questo re sono de oro e anche alcuna parte de la casa sua. Così ne riferitte lo medesimo re. Secondo lo suo costume, era molto in ordine e lo più bello uomo, che vedessimo tra questi popoli.*[18]
>
> (Pigafetta, 1956: 66)

Not only does Pigafetta confer individual subjectivity to an outstanding native, he acknowledges a potential prerequisite for civilisation, given that a recognisable sociopolitical stratification is central to Western political thought's conception of civilisation (Bowden, 2012). At this stage of European contact with the archipelago, the recurrent imagery of gold and material wealth in the *Relazione* is valuable to the economic ends of colonial conquest, which the civilising mission discursively legitimises (JanMohamed, 1985).

More than fifty years later, describing an already conquered yet still young colony, Carletti dissects the island's demography along religious lines as if to indicate the native groups' differing propensity to accept the Christian doctrine. He divides the archipelago between the Islamic *moros* and the heathen *bisaios*, likely subscribing to discursive norms of Spanish sources on the Philippine colony:

> *Tutta l'isola gira in circuito mille quattrocento miglia, poco piu o meno, molto bene abitata tutta di due sorte d'uomini Indiani: l'una, che gli Spagnoli chiamano Mori, per causa che, prima vi arrivassero li Cristiani d'Europa, v'erano ar rivati dall'Asia i ministri di Maometto, e questi*

> *avevano ricevuto il loro Alcorano e ne facevano religiosa proffessione; gli altri si adomandavano " bisaios ", nome proprio del paese, e questi si stavano ancora nella loro antica gentilità e idolatria, si come di presente molti stanno per mancamento di ministri che insegnino loro la verità del Evangelo.*[19]
>
> (Carletti, 1958: 91)

Those who are more susceptible to evangelisation are depicted by Carletti as whiter compared to the darker and "disfigured" Muslim natives, foregrounding the moral underpinnings of Western aesthetic ideals, which we already witnessed in Pigafetta's equation of beauty with fairness.

> *È questa natione molto differente dall'altra cosi in costumi come nella statura e gesti del corpo, essendo che li Mori sono piccoli e malfatti di viso e di corpo, e di colore assai bruno, e d'animo vile e poltrone; per contra questi altri hanno bella persona rubusta et virile, e molto piu bianchi di carnatura e piu valorosi nel maneggiar l'armi.*[20]
>
> (Carletti, 1958: 91)

This Manichean essentialisation of different native groups acquired a higher degree of specificity in the *Giro* as Gemelli Careri segments the "indians" according to regional origin in his chapter on "the Philippine Islands, its discovery, and the different Nations that populate it." Gemelli Careri, and to a lesser extent Carletti, had the advantage of an epistemological repertoire to draw from, which Pigafetta evidently did not.

As one might expect of textual representations of plural societies in the more advanced stages of Empire, Gemelli Careri's characterisation of the archipelago's various ethnolinguistic groups is rooted in their level of acceptance of colonial authority. Those who dared challenge the colonial masters are thus depicted in a negative light: "*La gente di Luban è iraconda; e data all'ubbriachezza. Ella fu la prima, che facesse resistenza agli Spagnuoli, con alcuni piccioli pezzi d'artiglieria, posti sopra un Forte*" (Gemelli Careri, 1700: 91).[21] Contrarily, those who have acclimatised to colonial rule are portrayed favourably: "*La gente [di Dimassivan] è di bastante capacità, ed ha due lodevoli costumi: l'uno d'ospiziarsi scambievolmente nel cammino; l'altro di non alterare il prezzo delle vittuaglie, per qualunque sterilità: e ciò sotto pene gravissime*"[22] (Gemelli Careri, 1700: 108). These "laudable" traits, however, read as a euphemism for subservience:

> *Vi sono circa 500 famiglie tributarie [nelle cinque Isole di Cuyo], più ragionevoli, ed amiche degli Spagnuoli, che quelle di Calamianes, e di Paragua. S'applicano grandemente alla fatica; e perciò raccolgono quantità grande di riso, di legumi, e d'altre frutta.*[23]
>
> (Gemelli Careri, 1700: 95–96)

That Gemelli Careri views the "indian's" degree of acculturation as an essential attribute is evidenced by the countless yet similar depictions of "barbarous" men without a sovereign. In the *Giro*, these "savages" refer to the ethnolinguistic groups, mostly residing in impenetrable mountains, that remained untouched by the "civilising" hand of colonial rule and who form part of the contemporary Philippines' recognised indigenous communities:

> *In tutto diversi, anzi contrari sono i Neri (Negrillos chiamati dagli Spagnuoli) che abitan nelle roccie, e ne' folti boschi, de' quali abbonda l'Isola di Manila. Eglino sono barbari, che si pascono di frutta, e di radici, che dà il monte, e di cacciagione, anche d'animali immondi, come sono scimmie, serpi, e sorci. . . . Non hanno leggi, nè lettere, nè altro Governo, ò Repubblica, che quello, che porta la parentela; imperocchè ubbidiscono tutti al Capo della famiglia. . . . Sono tanto nemici degli Spagnuoli, che, uccisone alcuno, invitano tutto il parentado; e per tre giorni fan festa, bevendo dentro quel cranio spolpato.*[24]
>
> (Gemelli Careri, 1700: 66–67)

The markers for civilisation are clearly identified. To not be a savage is to adhere to the Christian religion, to be governed – or possessed – by the Spaniards, to have a codified set of norms. While Gemelli Careri collectively categorises these "unruled" communities ("these blacks") as "savages" or "barbarians" who live like animals, he nevertheless acknowledges that one tribe is distinct from another by specifying their group name.

> *In più discorsi, avuti co' Padri della Compagnia, ed altri Missionari, (che trattano con questi Neri, Manghiani, Mundi, e Sambali) non mi fu mai possibile, per molta diligenza usata, sapere al loro Religione: anzi per lo contrario tutti concordemente diceano, che non ne hanno nissuna, e vivono da bestie.*[25]
>
> (Gemelli Careri, 1700: 68–69)

In their anthropological appraisal of the "Filipino" natives, only Gemelli Careri employs sub-humanising rhetoric in the form of animalistic similes: "*Partoriscono le donne di questi Satiri in mezzo a' boschi, a guisa di capre, e subito lavansi esse, e'l parto ne' fiumi o in altra ac- qua fredda: ciò che all'Europee causerebbe, senza alcun dubbio la morte*"[26] (Gemelli Careri, 1700: 68). Pigafetta takes part in this phenomenon of extreme othering, but solely with aborigines outside of the Philippine archipelago, such as his fantastic descriptions of the infamous giants of Patagonia, one of whom was hunted down and captured (read the Self practising what would be deemed as a barbaric action when actualised by the Other) by the Magellan crew with the intention of staging a spectacle in Europe. Just like in the *Relazione*, the marvellous trope surfaces in the *Giro*'s fifth volume with Gemelli Careri's description of a tailed, black indigene from the Mangyan tribe.[27] Carletti, by contrast, only attributed bestiality to native character and disposition rather than their physiognomy. However, neither in Pigafetta's *Relazione* nor in Carletti's *Ragionamenti* is any inhabitant of the archipelago directly likened to a beast. At first glance, Gemelli Careri may seem to deviate from homogenising rhetoric. He distinguishes between Christian "indians" (the Christianised natives) and Wild "indians" (the pagan blacks). He even distinguishes among the latter. Yet the emphasis that he places on the varying levels of acculturation, or rather, the different degrees of barbarism, serve only to support, even laud, the imperial civilising mission. In the final analysis, wild or tributary, Christianised or heathen, "indians" on the whole remain savages.

> *Io per me non credo, che vi siano Isole al Mondo più abbondanti. E in vero dove si troveranno monti, che sostentino tanta quantità d'uomini silvestri, colle sole frutta, e radici: che dano spontaneamente gli alberi, e'l terreno? poichè eglino in altro non s'adoprano, che nella cacciagione, e pure il lor novero è dieci volte più che' sudditi degli Spagnuoli.*[28]
>
> (Gemelli Careri, 1700: 119–120)

5.3 The implicit "we"

We have witnessed how all three chroniclers pursued the ethnographic impulse through their descriptions of the Philippine islanders. The publication of their chronicles transposed their semiotic creation in the fixity of print, launching the "Filipino" native into the Western imaginary. The textualisation of "they" is incorporated into a structure of knowledge and reproduced through "widely divergent rhetorical forms" (Spurr, 1993: 7). The three "Italian" chronicles all participated in colonial discourse but with varying degrees and modalities of othering dictated by the specific motives behind their travel and their own personal experiences during the journey. Pigafetta's unprecedented intercourse with the islanders and his assumed role as "participant observer" positioned him at an ethnographical junction: to represent the "Filipino" native in a way that arouses in the European reader the image of a "civilised" people or to maintain the extreme opposition of the "savage" and the "civilised." In his portrayal of "those people," Pigafetta rejects an extreme stance. He never says that "they are like us," only that "they have objects like ours" or that "they do things as we do them." The similarity between the native Other and the European observer never goes beyond what is perceptible to the naked eye as the "Filipino native" is ontologically Other.

Gemelli Careri is less ambivalent in his othering of colonial subjects. What we witness so evidently in his ethnographic notes on the diverse groups that populate the archipelago is a "transformation of racial difference into moral and even metaphysical difference" (JanMohamed, 1985: 61) as he intricately weaves descriptions of their exotic physical attributes with authoritative assessments of their character and moral code. We concur with Hester's (2016: 45) observation that Carletti assumed an ambiguous position as an external observer, whose impulse for travel did not derive from a "common sense of purpose and identity" (p. 45) yet whose interpretation of difference was nevertheless informed by a Catholic orientation and a Eurocentric worldview. But her insistence on the Italian lack of a proto-national identity[29] impeded her from lingering on the latter point, which constitutes an essential dimension of the entire operation of itinerant knowledge production, from the discovery of the New World to the global system's attendant transformations. Despite the heterogeneity of the colonial thesaurus, travel of Western provenance was always accompanied by text: "the aboriginal inhabitants . . . were seen through the lens of text and compared with the inhabitants of the ancient world" (Leed, 1991: 160).

Pigafetta, Carletti, and Gemelli Careri constitute a sense of identity through the imposition of an implicit "we" that is juxtaposed against "those people" or "those indians." In order to provide a more nuanced picture of their engagement with a practice that is often sweepingly perceived as colonial/European, it is necessary to problematise their conception of beyond the realm of poetics as Hester (2016) has already meticulously executed. In the *Relazione*, Pigafetta does not explicitly refer to Italy either as a point of departure or as a cultural reference. Curiously, two of the only three references to Italy in the *Relazione* deal with the voyager's re-entry. In his analysis of the Italian travellers' "placelessness," Cachey (1996) notes Italian literary identity's "constitutional lack of an original place either to depart from or to which return" (p. 59). While Italy might not be Pigafetta's *patria*, it does represent his site of repatriation and the stage of his professional "birthing"[30]:

> *e perchè ne l'esser mio in Italia, quando andava a la santità de papa Clemente, quella per sua grazia a Monteroso verso di me si dimostrò assai benigna e umana e dissemi che li sarebbe grato li copiassi tutte quelle cose [che] aveva viste e passate nella navigazione.*[31]
>
> (Pigafetta, 1956: 9)

The only other textual utterance of Italy is a comparison of modern-day Brazil's landmass with unified European states such as Spain and France,[32] which demonstrates Pigafetta's recognition of Italy as a geographical entity with territorial designation.

Written at the close of the sixteenth century, Carletti's *Ragionamenti* may be interpreted as the inauguration of a cosmopolitan Italian traveller whose autonomous activities highlight the increasing marginality of Italians in imperial domains. Even as Europe carved a space for the unique value of their textual production as "disinterested subjects," capable of offering or performing "objectivity," private globetrotters like Carletti and Gemelli Careri remained peripheral to their English, French, and Spanish counterparts (Hester, 2016: 156). Indeed, the travelling merchant reflected on the disadvantaged position he occupied as an "Italian" trader in Spanish-occupied territories and noted his own foreignness, not in relation to the indigenes encountered, but to European powers who monopolised commerce. In sum, Carletti was made aware of his own alterity as he travelled outside of the metropolis towards the imperially administered periphery or, as Spivak (1988) would contend, the "Italian" traveller in the midst of the radical Other was denied his "place in the seat of the Same or the Self" (p. 84).

> *E perché questi viaggi e navicationi dell'Indie non possono farsi d'altri, che dalla propria Natione Spagnola, noi come Italiani e forastieri venivamo a cascare in pregiuditio di perdere tutto l'avere che avessimo messo in un tal negotio, se mai si fusse saputo essere nostro.*[33]
>
> (Carletti, 1958: 8)

From the standpoint of postcolonial thought, Hester (2016) could have taken the opportunity to provide a more balanced contrapuntal reading of "Italian" explorers' textual production in the age of Empire, by teasing out the Bhabian tensions shaping the identity of globetrotting "Italians" obliged to perform Europeanness. Carletti's self-pronounced ambivalence is staged in the liminal space, that is, "in-between the designations of identity" (Bhabha, 1994: 4). Any subject in motion is already, by virtue of his/her passage from one fixed point to another, a liminal figure. The traveller oscillates between a community to which he is alleged and another to which he is a stranger (Leed, 1991: 59). The Florentine merchant's own words ("*noi come Italiani e forastieri*") entreat scholars to read the liminality that shapes the subjectivity of cosmopolitan "Italian" travel writers. Rather than fixate on their Otherness within Europe or leap to the opposite extreme by homogenising them as Othering agents of the Imperial West, their shifting positionalities can take centre stage in our reading of their chronicles.

Of the three Italian travelogues, Carletti's seamless identity manoeuvring most clearly exemplifies the cosmopolitan "Italian's" liminality. The Florentine merchant understood the vulnerability of his position as a private trader as opposed to the Spanish merchants he encountered in Peru or the Portuguese traders in Java, who enjoyed the protection of their monarchs (Guglielminetti, 2015: 16). The intricate bureaucracy behind global commerce required him to declare his nationality which, depending on a given locality's relationship to imperial power, might cost him considerable expenses or even prove fatal to the continuation of his journey.

> *Ma per non avere a contendere ogni volta che andavamo da un luogo all'altro con li nuovi ministri del Re, deputato per le suddette compositioni, si compose solo mio padre per cinquecento reali, che possono valere*

> *quaranta cinque scudi, e in questo il Governatore di Cartagena si portò amichevolmente; per mio conto non si fece altra compositione, perché passavo per tutto come Spagnolo.*[34]
>
> (Carletti, 1958: 30–31)

He would therefore identify, or let himself be identified, as either European (imperial Spanish) or Italian (free national) based on geopolitical calculations.

> *Noi rispondemmo esser venuti dall'isole Filippine a quelle del Giappone e poi in questa d'Amacao, di dove era nostro pensiero e desiderio passare all'India orientale, per nostro spasso e curiosità e non per altro interesse o altro che contrafacesse o preterisse alli ordini regi dell'una né dell'altra Corona; inoltre ch'eramo di natione Italiana e che venivamo d'un paese libero, come era il Giappone, non apunto soggetto né all'una né all'altra natione Spagnola, e che l'andare per il mondo era cosa che si permetteva a tutte le nationi.*[35]
>
> (Carletti, 1958: 153)

The commercial motive behind his travel, circumscribed neither within conquest nor mere exploration, behoved Carletti to acknowledge the semiotic instability of national boundaries. His primary interest, after all, was to ensure his mobility in contested grounds. To make his way through the labyrinthine routes of the New World rife with political and bureaucratic traps, Carletti's "we" discourse is unstable, dislodged from fixity, and suspended in the liminal space of in-betweenness, as he himself declared: "*noi, che non eramo né di questi né di quelli*" 'we, who were neither these nor those' (Carletti, 1958: 78). His Italy, just as in the *Relazione* beforehand and in the *Giro* afterwards, is a geographical entity. It is the starting point of his venture,[36] but not his place of provenance. He is, first and foremost, a "*cittadino fiorentino*" (Carletti, 1958: 268), and the Grand Duchy of Tuscany his sole institutional protector. His vision, too, of a "free Italian nation similar to Japan" (Carletti, 1958: 153) could have been said of the Florentine Republic but not did not hold water for Gemelli Careri's southern Italian birthplace.

Despite the shorter temporal distance that bridges his account from that of Carletti's, Gemelli Careri's "we" discourse in the *Giro*'s fifth volume is more akin to Pigafetta's, as it appears to be circumscribed in a broader European context rather than a specifically Italian provenance. Even though images of Italy do occasionally emerge from his testimony, these textual instances do not reveal any cultural grounding to *italianità*, except for a single parenthetical mention of Italian architecture when describing a church.[37] The few other Italian references in his Philippine voyage are geological (citing the ancient peninsula's geological formation),[38] meteorological (comparing Philippine heat with Italian climate),[39] or as a mere setting to an Albanian custom.[40] This mirrored Pigafetta's recognition of Italy as a geographical entity. In the same vein, Gemelli Careri's intertexual methodology excludes Italian sources. As we know, Gemelli Careri made explicit references to previous travel and historical documents in order to fill the gaps in his time-bound observations. A substantial amount of literature about the Philippine Islands had already been published prior to the author's visit, yet just like Carletti overlooked Pigafetta, so did Gemelli Careri scarcely mention his "Italian" predecessors. Nelli (2009) notes this particularity, observing that in the six volumes comprising the *Giro*, Italian chroniclers were scarcely represented, even though the author's innovative intertextuality included explicit credits to previous chroniclers. It is impossible to know whether it was wilful omission on the author's part, only that it would be a gross oversight considering his self-fashioning as a learned traveller who recommends studying all extant chronicles about one's destinations. Like Gemelli Careri, Carletti also failed to mention Pigafetta's role in textualising the earliest European–Philippine contact even in his introduction of the discovery and subsequent colonisation of the Islands in the Philippine part of his *Ragionamenti*.

Travelling one century later, Gemelli Careri occupied the same liminal space that Carletti had done as a European globetrotter who did not belong to a consolidated nation in zones of alterity subject to imperial power. Yet instead of shifting positionalities to suit his needs as they arose, the Calabrian traveller, of the three chroniclers under scrutiny, performed the rhetoric of Empire with the least ambiguity. Not only did he employ essentialising and homogenising strategies in his ethnography, Gemelli Careri also adopted extreme modes of othering such as the sub-humanisation of the "barbarous" indigenes, mirroring the famed Jesuit theologian's judgment: "*el indio es irracional; es, en fin, animal*" 'the Indian is irrational; he is, in the end, animal' (Acosta, 1575–1576 [1984]: 139–141). Although Pigafetta should not be exempt from Bhabian contrapuntal reading, his cosmopolitan intellectualism in service of the Empire has more resonance with his predecessor Columbus than his autonomous successors. The ushering of an autonomous travel writing by cosmopolitan Italians, inaugurated by Carletti in 1594 and followed by Gemelli Careri in 1699, heightened the liminality of "Italian" intellectuals in a way that Pigafetta had circumvented as his travel was mandated by a colonial power. Unlike his successors, he can thus be understood to have written under the aegis of Empire. This is how he concludes the preeminent testimony of the first circumnavigation of the globe before his repatriation:

> *Me ne partii de lì al meglio [che] potei; e andai in Portogallo e parlai al re don Giovanni de le cose [che] aveva vedute. Passando per la Spagna venni in Franza; e feci dono de alcune cose de l'altro emisfero a la madre del cristianissimo re don Francesco, madama la reggente. Poi me ne venni ne la Italia, ove donai per sempre me medesimo e queste mie poche fatiche*

> *a lo inclito e illustrissimo signor Filippo de Villers Lisleadam, gran maestro de Rodi dignissimo.*[41]
>
> (Pigafetta, 1956: 223–234)

We might recall that pre-Unification Italians were themselves suspended in the fixity of print as European observers flocked to Italy during the Grand Tour. Like the natives of the Philippine Islands, the inhabitants of the Italian peninsula were also textualised by foreign beholders of the gaze, represented through an "abstract" they, and essentialised in that their actions, customs, and traditions were interpreted as a function of their nature. Incidentally, the "Italian" Other was also portrayed by European observers as indolent and pleasure-seeking.

> *In Europa circolano descrizioni negative degli italiani almeno dalla fine del Medioevo quando non era affatto raro che i banchieri e i mercanti lombardi e fiorentini venissero accusati di avarizia, irreligiosità, lussuria e disonestà. . . . Anche la vasta letteratura del Grand Tour fece la sua parte, consolidando un proprio assortimento di immagini e stereotipi poco lusinghieri: spesso i viaggiatori descrivevano gli abitanti della penisola come individui indolenti, moralmente e sessualmente disinvolti, facili a menare le mani e a ricorrere al coltello, malgrado altrettanto spesso trovassero aspetti piacevoli proprio in alcuni di questi atteggiamenti.*[42]
>
> (Patriarca, 2010: 4)

As the "Italian" travellers ventured away from a de-territorialised homeland towards conquered spaces, they reproduced this rhetoric, revealing a shifting positionality from Othered to Othering subjects. Their textual production thus represents an interstitial zone, perpetuating this epistemic operation as they moved from their liminal space in the peripherical centre to the extreme periphery. Still, we must be wary of homogenising not just discourses of Otherness but the very production of these discourses.

Analysing travel writing during the Grand Tour, Bideaux (1996) points to two major characteristics defining the episteme of voyage to Italy, namely "*discernment dans la perception, équité dans le jugement*" 'understanding in perception, fairness in judgment' (p. 90). Did Pigafetta, Carletti, and Gemelli Careri adopt this epistemic framework as they interpreted and represented "Filipino" alterity? We argue that the same equitable judgment could not have been extended to the radically different Others of far-flung territories whom Spivak (1988) considers to be casualties of a veritable epistemic violence. As the three displaced chroniclers narrativised their encounters with the peoples of the Philippine archipelago, they simultaneously participated in the construction of native subjectivity to legitimise the colonial enterprise and consolidated their own fragmented subjectivity to validate their belongingness to the European cosmopolis. Notwithstanding their ambiguous status in the home continent because of the linguistic, cultural, and political fragmentation of their homeland, the "Italian" explorers could not have suffered subalternity. The very act of writing about their travels to the Orient, inscribed within the framework of European exploration, attests to their capacity for speech. Indeed, the interrogation of the "Italian" chroniclers' representation of the "Filipino" native reveals how these itinerant Italians possessed the capacity to shift their positionality as Subject.

Notes

1 Inasmuch as, most illustrious and excellent Lord, there are many curious persons who not only take pleasure in knowing and hearing the great and wonderful things that God has permitted me to see and suffer during my long and dangerous voyage, herein described, but who also wish to know the means and manners and paths that I have taken in making that voyage; and who do not lend full credence to the end unless they have a perfect assurance of the beginning (Pigafetta, 2007: 3).
2 All joyfully entreated the captain to leave them two men, or at least one, to instruct them in the faith, and [said] that they would show them great honour. The captain replied to them that he could not leave them any men then, but that if they wished to become Christians, our priest would baptize them, and that he would next time bring priests and friars who would instruct them in our faith. They answered that they would first speak to their king, and that then they would become Christians. We all wept with great joy (Pigafetta, 2007: 45).
3 [A]nd being taught by customs to endure the fatigues of long voyages, I resolv'd without any demur to sail from Macao to the Philippine Islands . . . in order to expose myself afterwards, to the most dangerous voyage that can possibly be imagin'd, in which for seven months, I was toss'd by most boisterous and frightful storms (Gemelli Careri, 1963: 1).
4 So great is the dignity and excellency of human nature, and so active those sparks of heavenly fire it partakes of, that they ought to be look'd upon as very mean, and unworthy the name of men, who thro' pusilanimity, by them call'd prudence, or through sloath, which they stile moderation, or else through avarice, to which they give the name of frugality, at any rate withdraw themselves from great and noble actions. Many make it their business to extol the glorious undertakings of others, both in verse and prose; and yet very few will attempt those things that may purchase them such praise (Gemelli Careri, 1963: 1).
5 In the original Italian, Pigafetta alternates between "*popoli*" 'peoples' and "*gente*" 'people' with no apparent distinction.
6 Having taken our leave of him, the prince took us with him to his house, where four young girls were playing [instruments]: one, on a drum like ours, but resting on the ground; the second was striking two suspended metal discs alternately with a stick made thick at the end with palm cloth wrapped around it; the third, one large metal disc in the same manner (Pigafetta, 2007: 47).

7 Those girls were very beautiful and almost as white as our girls and as large; they were naked except for tree cloth hanging from the waist and reaching to the knees, and some were quite naked and had large holes in their ears with a small round piece of wood in the hole, which keeps the hole round and large, and they have long black hair, and wear a short cloth about the head, and are always barefoot (Pigafetta, 2007: 47).

8 Those people go naked, wearing but one piece of palm-tree cloth about their private parts. The males, both young and old, have their penis pierced from one side to the other near the head, with a gold or tin bolt. . . . I very often asked many, both old and young, to see their penis, because I could not believe it. . . . They say that their women wish it so, and that if they did otherwise they would not have intercourse with them. When the men wish to have intercourse with their women, the women themselves take the penis, not in the regular way, and commence very gently to introduce it [into their vagina], with the spur on top first, and then the other part. When it is inside it takes its regular position; and thus the penis always stays inside until it gets soft, for otherwise they could not pull it out. Those people make use of that device because they are of a weak nature (Pigafetta, 2007: 54–55).

9 They have as many wives as they wish, but one of them is the principal wife. Whenever any of our men went ashore, both by day and by night, they invited him to eat and to drink. Their viands are half cooked and very salty; they drink frequently and copiously from the jars through those small reeds, and one of their meals lasts for five or six hours. The women loved us very much more than their own men. All of the women from the age of six years and upward have their vaginas gradually opened because of the men's penises (Pigafetta, 2007: 55).

10 The *bisaio* men are all very much given to the pleasures of Venus, and their women are no less ardent than beautiful, and they beguile themselves with these women in strange and diabolic ways. And especially one way that I should not dare to relate to Your Serene Highness if I had not seen it myself, not wishing to be taken for a liar. But as, out of curiosity and to be certain about it, I also spent some money to be showed what I had been told about, you therefore can rely upon me. These *bisaios*, or most of them, by an invention of the Devil and so as to give and receive diabolic pleasure with their women, have the custom of making a hole in their membrum virile. . . . This method of having lustful pleasure was, they say, devised by them for reasons of health, that is, to have fewer occasions to make use of venery and to have their women more sated. But I also heard it said that, on the contrary, that is pure invention of Satan, done to impede those wretched people from generating children (Carletti, 1964: 83–84).

11 "they spend their time, arranging fights between cocks" (Carletti, 1964: 83).

12 "The *bisaio* men are all very much given to the pleasures of Venus" (Carletti, 1964: 83).

13 They played so harmoniously that it appeared they had great knowledge of music (Pigafetta, 2007: 47).

14 And those Indians who were swimming in the sea, not letting themselves be seen because of fear of our arquebus shots, hid themselves beneath our ship, coming to the surface of the water sometimes on one side, sometimes on the other, in order to get their breath. And then, suddenly, they would plunge back, in that being such excelling swimmers that they had nothing for which to envy fish. . . . Certainly that is an act of marvelous dexterity and amazement. But is it a marvel, seeing that those men are always out on the sea and live by fishing in it? Or it may be, as there were many to say, that they do it by means of witchcraft or incantations? (Carletti, 1964: 75–76)

15 It is their laziness, that makes them appear less ingenious; and they are so entirely addicted to it, that if in walking they find a thorn run into their foot, they will not stoop to put it out of the way, that another may not tread on it (Gemelli Careri, 1963: 47).

16 Since the Spaniards rule over them, they are grown lazy; they are good at mechanicks, as for instance at making chains, and curious beads of gold, and other things (Gemelli Careri, 1963: 47).

17 Rizal would publish the essay, *Sobre la indolencia de los filipinos* (1890), two centuries later, in which he linked the oft-cited native malady to demotivation under an unrewarding, oppressive colonial rule.

18 Pieces of gold of the size of walnuts and eggs are found by sifting the earth in the island of that king who came to our ships. All the dishes of that king are of gold and also some portion of his house, as the king himself told us. According to their customs he was very grandly decked out, and the most handsome man that we saw among those people (Pigafetta, 2007: 37).

19 The entire island measures 1,400 miles around, more or less, and is well populated, entirely by two sorts of Indians: one sort whom the Spaniards call *moros* because, before the Christians arrived from Europe, the ministers of Mohammed had arrived from Asia and these people had received their Koran and professed that religion; and the others, whom they call *bisaios*, a name native to the country, and these are people who still preserved their ancient genteelness and idolatry, as many still retain them because of a lack of ministers to teach them the truth of the Evangel (Carletti, 1964: 83).

20 The latter nation differs greatly from the other both in customs and in bodily gestures. The moros are small and badly formed in face and body, of a very brown color and of base and lazy spirit. On the contrary, those others have beautiful bodies, robust and virile, and are much whiter in complexion (Carletti, 1964: 83).

21 "The people of Luban are passionate and given to drunkenness. It was the first that oppos'd the Spaniards with a few pieces of canon planted on a fort" (Gemelli Careri, 1963: 4).

22 "The people of [Dimassivan] are susceptible of any learning, and have two good customs, the one to travel, the other never to alter the price of provisions upon any dearth, and this under severe penalties" (Gemelli Careri, 1963: 52).

23 In the [five islands of Cuyo] there are about 500 tributary families, more civiliz'd, and better affected to Spaniards than those of Calamianes and

Palawan. They are very laborious and gather an abundance of rice, grain and other fruit (Gemelli Careri, 1963: 46).

24 The blacks, by the Spaniards, call'd Negrillos, who live on the mountains and in thick woods, whereof there is plenty in Manila, differ quite from all the rest. They are mere Barbarians, and feed on such fruits and roots, as the mountains afford, and upon all they can kill, even to monkeys, snakes, and rats. . . . They have no laws, letters or government, but that which kindred makes, for they all obey the head of their family. . . . They are such enemies to the Spaniards, that if they happen to kill one, they invite all their kindred, and rejoice for three days drinking out of [that] skull, clear'd for that purpose (Gemelli Careri, 1963: 32).

25 Tho' I had much discourse about it, with the fathers of the Society, and other missioners, who converse with these blacks, Manghians, Mandi, and Sambali, I could never learn anything of their religion; but on the contrary, all unanimously agree that they have none, but live like beasts (Gemelli Careri, 1963: 33).

26 The wives of those [Satyrs] are deliver'd in the woods like she goats, and immediately wash themselves of the infants in the rivers, or the cold water; which would be immediate death to Europeans (Gemelli Careri, 1963: 58).

27 "*Mi dissero alcuni Padri della Compagnia, degni di fede, che questi Manghiani, tengono un palmo di coda nella parte posteriore*" (Gemelli Careri, 1700: 90).

28 I am of the opinion that there are not such plentiful islands in the world. For where shall we find mountains that will maintain such a number of savage men with their fruit, and roots naturally produced by the tree, and soil; for they apply themselves to nothing but shooting, and their number is ten times more than the subjects of the Spaniards (Gemelli Careri, 1963: 58).

29 See Hodorowich (2009) for a critique of Hester's (2016) subscription to the "too-teleological narrative" of Italy's decadence as nonconformant to the traditional European nationhood narrative.

30 "*[C]he . . . potessero partorirme qualche nome appresso la posterità*" (Pigafetta, 1956: 8).

31 And inasmuch as when I was in Italy and going to see His Holiness Pope Clement, you by your grace showed yourself very kind and good to me at Monterosi, and told me that you would be pleased if I would copy down for you all those things that I had seen and suffered during the voyage (Pigafetta, 2007: 4).

32 "*Questa terra del Verzin è abbondantissima e più grande che la Spagna, Franza e Italia tutte insieme: è del re de Portugallo*" (Pigafetta, 1956: 18).

33 And because voyages and navigation in the Indies could not be made by men not subjects of the Spanish nation itself, we as Italians and foreigners fell under the shadow of losing all the possessions we had out into that commerce if they ever should become known as being ours (Carletti, 1964: 4).

34 Every time we went from one place to another, in order not to have to contend with new ministers of the King, in charge of the aforementioned

commercial taxes, only my father paid the five-hundred *reali* charge, which is likely worth forty-five *scudi*, wherefore the Governor of Cartagena behaved amicably; for my part, no commercial taxes were paid because I passed for a Spaniard.

35 We replied that we had come from the Philippine Islands to Japan and then to this island of Amacao, through which we thought of and desired to transit towards eastern India, for our amusement and curiosity and not for any other interest or anything else that betrayed or transgressed the royal orders of either Crown; furthermore, that we were from the Italian nation and that we came from a free country, such as Japan, not subject to either the Spanish nation or another, and that going around the world was something permitted to all the nations.

36 "*[P]artendo d'Italia per Spagna e di quivi per via dell'Indie nuove, insino all'essere arrivato in quest'isole Filippine*" '[D]eparting from Italy for Spain and from there to the New Indies, until having arrived in the Philippine Islands' (Carletti, 1958: 103).

37 "*L'Altar maggiore è in forma di mezzo circolo (che gli Architetti Italiani direbbono alla Borromina) tutto bene adorno di colonne, e di bellissimi intagli, riccamente dorati; che maggiormente risplendono per la vicina cupola!*" (Gemelli Careri, 1700: 27).

38 "*[C]ome si dice essere avvenuto alla Sicilia, già per lo passato congiunta colla terra ferma d'Italia; all'Isola di Cipro, ch'era attaccata alla Soria, e ad altre*" (Gemelli Careri, 1700: 31).

39 "*Il temperamento d'aria nelle Filippine è generalmente caldo, ed umido. Il caldo non è così sensibile come quello de' giorni canicolari in Italia; però più penoso*" (Gemelli Careri, 1700: 55).

40 "*Le donne portano i bambini entro bisaccie, fatte di scorze d'alberi; o ligati con un panno, come usano in Italia alcuni Albanesi*" (Gemelli Careri, 1700: 33).

41 I left there as best I could and went to Portugal, where I spoke with King Dom João of what I had seen. Passing through Spain, I went to France, where I made a gift of certain things from the other hemisphere to the mother of the most Christian king, Don Francis, Madame the Regent. Then I came to Italy, where I devoted myself forever, and these my poor labours, to the famous and most illustrious Lord Philippe de Villiers l'Isle-Adam, the most worthy Grand Master of Rhodes (Pigafetta, 1956: 126).

42 In Europe, towards the end of the Middle Ages, there was such a widespread depiction of Italians in a negative light that it was not at all strange for Lombard and Florentine bankers and merchants to be accused of greed, being unreligious, and dishonesty. The vast literature of the Grand Tour also contributed greatly, consolidating a mass of unflattering images and stereotypes. Most often, travellers described the peninsula's inhabitants as indolent people, morally and sexually insolent, taken to violence on a knife-edge, despite often finding pleasant aspects of some of these qualities.

Reference list

Acosta, J. (1575–1576 [1987]). *De procuranda indorum salute: Educación y evangelización*. Madrid: CSIC Press.

Ashcroft, B., Griffiths, G., & Tiffin, H. (2013). *Post-colonial studies: The key concepts*. Routledge.

Bhabha, H. (1994). *The location of culture*. Routledge.

Bideaux, M. (1996). Le Voyage d'Italie, instrument de la connaissance de soi par la fréquentation d'autrui. *Annali d'Italianistica*, *14*, 89–102.

Bowden, B. (2012). Politics in a world of civilizations: long-term perspectives on relations between peoples. *Human Figurations*, *1*(2).

Buccini, S. (1996). Coerenza metodologica nel "Giro del mondo" di Giovanni Francesco Gemelli Careri. *Annali d'Italianistica*, *14*, 246–256.

Cachey, T. J. (1996). An Italian literary history of travel. *Annali d'Italianistica*, *14*, 55–64.

Carletti, F. (1958). *Ragionamenti del mio viaggio al mondo*. Giulio Einaudi editore.

De Acosta, J., & Mateos, F. (1999). *Predicación del Evangelio en las Indias*. Biblioteca Virtual Miguel de Cervantes.

Field, R. J. (2006). Revisiting Magellan's voyage to the Philippines. *Philippine Quarterly of Culture and Society*, *34*(4), 313–337.

Gemelli Careri, G. F. (1700). *Giro del mondo del dottor d. Gio. Francesco Gemelli Careri* (Vol. 5, *contenente le cose più ragguardevoli vedute nell'Isole*). Giuseppe Roselli.

Guglielminetti, M. (Ed.). (2015). *Viaggiatori del seicento*. Utet Libri.

Hester, N. (2003). Geographies of belonging: Italian travel writing and Italian identity in the age of early European tourism. *Annali d'Italianistica. Hodoeporics Revisited/Ritorno all'odeporica*, *21*, 287–300.

Hester, N. (2011). Mapping Petrarch in seventeenth-century Italian travel writing. *Humanist Studies & the Digital Age*, *1*(1), 128–135.

Hester, N. (2016). *Literature and identity in Italian baroque travel writing*. Routledge.

JanMohamed, A. R. (1985). The economy of Manichean allegory: The function of racial difference in colonialist literature. *Critical inquiry*, *12*(1), 59–87.

Jasinski, J. (2001). *Sourcebook on rhetoric*. Sage Publications.

Jones, R. B. (2011). *Postcolonial representations of women: Critical issues for education* (Vol. 18). Springer Science & Business Media.

Leed, E. J. (1991). *The mind of the traveller. From Gilgamesh to global tourism*. Basic Books.

Loureiro, R. (2014). Traveling experiences vs. intertextuality. *Anais de História de Além-Mar*, *15*, 101–136.

Meiu, G. P. (2015). Colonialism and sexuality. *The international encyclopedia of human sexuality*, *1*, 197–290.

Mojares, R. B. (2002). *Waiting for mariang makiling: Essays in Philippine cultural history*. Ateneo University Press.

Monga, L. (1996). Travel and travel writing: An historical overview of hodoeporics. *Annali d'italianistica*, *14*, 6–54.

Motsch, A. (2011). Relations of travel: Itinerary of a practice. *Renaissance and Reformation/Renaissance et Réforme*, 207–236.
Nelli, R. (2009, April 2). Giovanni Francesco Gemelli Careri e la Nuova Spagna. Genesi, fortuna e struttura di un testo. Fundación Canaria Orotava de Historia de la Ciencia. *Ciencia y cultura entre dos mundos. Nueva España y Canarias como ejemplos de Knowledge in Transit*. https://fundacionorotava.org/publicaciones/actas-de-congresos/ciencia-y-cultura-entre-dos-mundos/
Patriarca, S. (2010). *Italianità: la costruzione del carattere nazionale*. Gius. Laterza & Figli.
Perocco, D. (1997). *Viaggiare e raccontare: Narrazione di viaggio ed esperienze di racconto tra Cinque e Seicento*. Edizioni dell'Orso.
Pigafetta, A. (1956). Relazione del primo viaggio intorno al mondo. In C. Manfroni (Ed.), *Collana viaggi esplorazioni scoperte*. Istituto editoriale italiano.
Pigafetta, A. (2007). In T. J. Cachey, L. Ballerini, & M. Ciavolella (Eds.), *First voyage around the world (1519–1522): An account of Magellan's expedition*. University of Toronto Press.
Porter, D. (2015). Orientalism and its problems. In P. Williams & L. Chrisman (Eds.), *Colonial discourse and post-colonial theory* (pp. 150–161). Routledge.
Pratt, M. L. (1985). Scratches on the face of the country; Or, what Mr. Barrow saw in the land of the bushmen. *Critical Inquiry*, *12*(1), 119–143.
Rabasa, J. (1993). *Inventing America: Spanish historiography and the formation of Eurocentrism* (Vol. 11). University of Oklahoma Press.
Rubiés, J. P. (2002). Travel writing and ethnography. In P. D. Hulme (Ed.), *The Cambridge companion to travel writing* (pp. 242–260). Cambridge University Press.
Silvestro, G. (1958). Introduzione. In F. Carletti, *Ragionamenti del mio viaggio intorno al mondo* (pp. VII–XIV). Einaudi.
Sloterdijk, P. (2013). *In the world interior of capital: Towards a philosophical theory of globalization*. Polity.
Spurr, D. (1993). *The rhetoric of empire. Colonial discourse in journalism, travel writing, and imperial administration*. Duke University Press.
Testa-de Ocampo, A. M. (2010). The marvelous turn in the accounts of the Magellan expedition to the Philippines in the 16th century. *Journal of English Studies and Comparative Literature*, *10*(1).
Young, R. J. C. (1995). *Colonial desire: Hybridity in theory, culture and race*. Routledge.

Conclusion

Travel is not merely an act; it is also a text. And like any text, it is produced through the dynamic interplay of social, cultural, and historical contexts. That early modern Europe saw an overzealous, unprecedented publication of travel narrations was both a fundamental component and an inevitable consequence of the era's geopolitical configurations. Hence, chronicles of one's travel can be read to exist in a dialectical relationship with the context of their genesis as they are simultaneously products and producers of certain ways of being, thinking, and exercising power. The rise of modern states across the continent ran parallel with its emerging hegemonic status in view of the Western European zeitgeist that ascribed expansionist ideals to the consolidation of the nation. This expansionist project, in turn, birthed the discourse of difference that would be (re)produced through the agency of travel writers. Travel as journey was the foremost means by which conquest was waged and commerce conducted while travel as text was an indispensable tool in reimagining and reshaping the globe and its diverse denizens. The repertoire of Modernity is replete with travel reports doubling as ethnographic accounts of innumerable native communities in the New World and the Far East. Of the vast colonial repository, this study zeroed in on Italian travel writing about the Philippine archipelago throughout its colonial history and presented two approaches which need not be divorced from one another. The first drew insights from postcolonial criticism, with particular focus on the construction of the Othered subject in the three accounts. The latter framed their chronicles within the context of travel as a prevalent yet noncanonical genre in the Italian literary tradition, and of Italy's historical ambivalence in early modern Europe. Both lines of inquiry foreground the intricate relationship between place and identity construction that transpires in travel writing, while revealing travel writing's place not just in the colonial infrastructure of knowledge but also in counter-hegemonic articulations of the nation, such as the Gramscian postulate of an Italian nationhood situated in its international European function and the deployment and contestation of Western episteme by the anticolonial Filipino Propaganda Movement.

DOI: 10.4324/9781032722320-7

Since the collapse of the Roman Empire, the territorially disintegrated Italian peninsula lent itself to foreign rule and consequently witnessed a steady decline in its role in continental geopolitics and, by extension, its influence in the engineering of Western "civilisation." Splintered into destabilised *staterelli*, with each proto-state developing or stagnating at an unequal rate, Italy was driven to the periphery, driving a significant number of skilled and educated individuals abroad to maximise their faculties either independently or in the service of a foreign power. In this context, Italian knowledge production assumed a cosmopolitan character and purpose. The three chroniclers examined in this book were among these itinerant Italians. Antonio Pigafetta, Francesco Carletti, and Giovanni Francesco Gemelli Careri, originating from different political, literary, and linguistic contexts, travelled away from Europe's internal Other into the wider world where they would encounter aborigines in different stages of conquest and assimilation into the Western colonial venture. Their voyages allowed them to observe elements of indigenous life which they would scrupulously document in writing and recount to their respective patrons upon their return to the Old World. Considering that ethnography is an essential component of the literary genre of travel, "Italian" travel narrators hence participated, consciously or unwittingly, in the expansion and validation of asymmetric power structures through the dissemination of knowledge about colonial subjects.

Pigafetta, Carletti, and Gemelli Careri performed the rhetoric of imperial Europe as they came in contact with radically different cultures at various historical conjunctures. Notwithstanding the near century that separates each account from one another, there are recognisable parallelisms in the way that they paint the image of the "Filipino" native. All three assume an essentialising tone as they represent the Philippine islanders into an abstract "they" and interpret their actions as a function of their innate nature, completely devoid of context or historicity. Pigafetta indirectly summons the prospective colonisers by painting an alluring picture of a hospitable, peaceful people given to leisure and idleness. Carletti corroborates many of his predecessor's impressions, while his inventory of the island's resources and religiously laden assessment of indigenous culture seems to invite deeper colonial intervention. Gemelli Careri legitimises the colonial mission by conjuring up an image of an abundant archipelago peopled by different groups of "indians" with varying degrees of savagery, a condition which is inversely proportional to their degree of subservience and acculturation to the colonial regime. The rhetorical conventions employed by all three travellers facilitate the act of ascribing deviant characteristics to the natives, which ultimately serve to legitimise Modernity's civilising mission. Pigafetta's and Carletti's narratives are tinged with undertones of exoticisation and can be interpreted as gentler when juxtaposed with Gemelli Careri's overt attribution of barbaric traits to the natives.

Studying these "Italian" chroniclers' semiotic creation of "those people" or "those Indians" revealed an affirmation of the Other's ontological inferiority. This begets the question: who are "we" whom "they" are inferior to? Indeed, the discursive construction of "they" always implies the constitution of an unconscious "we." While visions of Italy do emerge from each chronicle, they are not only few and far between but are also suggestive of a mere geographical conception rather than a cultural grounding. Pigafetta's and Gemelli Careri's "we"-discourses were markedly inscribed within the continental rather than the (proto)national. In contrast, Carletti's implicit "we" more acutely represented the "Italian" traveller's liminality, since he fashioned himself according to his exigencies. Depending on convenience, he would either identify as belonging to the free "nation" of Italy or let himself be identified as a subject of an imperial power. Accorded the privilege of travelling aboard the historically significant Magellan–Elcano expedition, Pigafetta shared a sense of purpose and common identity with the Spanish imperial enterprise and conveyed utmost devotion to the Portuguese captain. Gemelli Careri's innovative intertextual methodology, combined with his literary ambitions, resulted in a voluminous account which reproduced and supplemented European textual production on native ontology. Carletti's feelings of marginality as an independent trader in colonial domains informed his disenchanted gaze, which still did not preclude Eurocentric value judgments of indigenous customs. Indeed, all three read and represented "Filipino" alterity through the lens of European civilisation.

Although literary historians have begun elaborating travel literature of "Italian" provenance as a contrapuntal reading to European colonial literature, the "Italian" traveller's ambiguous subjectivity in the Age of Empire has not been adequately elucidated in Bhabian terms. As Pigafetta, Carletti, and Gemelli Careri uprooted themselves, we can perceive in their respective accounts an ambivalent sense of provenance. This is a less radical take compared to previous readings of a profound Italian cultural anxiety triggered by a "historic sense of placelessness." We argue, instead, that "place" itself is not a stable category and can thus be situated in the liminal. By viewing postcolonial thought and the "troubled" Italian national identity as mutually exclusive domains of analysis, previous studies ironically suspend these "Italian" subjects in the fixity of "placelessness," reducing their agency in the production of other subjectivities. On the other hand, the prevalent narrative in Philippine historiography tends to read colonial-era travel literature as a monolithic discourse and fails to incorporate the specific subjectivities of the so-called agents of Empire in their conceptual frameworks. All this considered, the novel contribution of this monograph on Italian travel writing about colonial Philippines is the opening of an analytical middle ground, highlighting the ambivalence of Italian chroniclers while acknowledging their participation in epistemological practices subsumed within the broader enterprise of conquest. There is no shortage of travel accounts of "Italian" provenance from which counter-hegemonic discourses can be teased out. This book's contrapuntal reading of Italian travel at the Age of Empire may be applied to other colonial spaces and contexts not just to investigate the distinct manifestations of the "Italian" travellers' unique subjectivity but also to probe other subalterns' engagements, if any, with itinerant knowledge production.

Index

For Product Safety Concerns and Information please contact our EU
representative GPSR@taylorandfrancis.com
Taylor & Francis Verlag GmbH, Kaufingerstraße 24, 80331 München, Germany

www.ingramcontent.com/pod-product-compliance
Lightning Source LLC
LaVergne TN
LVHW010939110826
845149LV00013B/2676

* 9 7 8 1 0 3 2 7 2 2 3 0 6 *